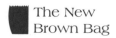
The New
Brown Bag

Show Me a Picture

 The New
Brown Bag

Show Me a Picture
30 Children's Sermons
Using Visual Art

Phyllis Vos Wezeman

Anna L. Liechty

THE
PILGRIM
PRESS
Cleveland

To Elizabeth "Lib" Segal . . .

. . . whose focus on justice has helped many people envision God's picture of peace for the world.

—*(P.V.W.)*

In memory of Clara Betz . . .

. . . an artist who taught me the joy of self-expression.

—*(A.L.L.)*

The Pilgrim Press, 700 Prospect Avenue East, Cleveland, Ohio 44115-1100
thepilgrimpress.com

09 08 07 06 05   5 4 3 2 1

Library of Congress Cataloging-in-Publication Data

Wezeman, Phyllis Vos.
    Show me a picture : 30 children's sermons using visual art / Phyllis Vos Wezeman ; Anna L. Liechty.
        p.   cm.   (The new brown bag)
    Includes bibliographical references.
    ISBN 0-8298-1636-4 (alk. paper)
    1. Children's sermons.   2. Church year sermons.   3. Christianity and art.
I. Liechty, Anna L.   II. Title.   III. Series.

BV4315.W434 2005
252'.53—dc22

2005022477

Contents

Overview

What is this book?

Show Me A Picture: 30 Children's Sermons Using Visual Art is a collection of messages primarily designed for use with kindergarten through upper-elementary youth. This resource addresses the special days of the liturgical calendar from a variety of approaches. While each sermon is based on a Scripture passage or verse, the message also incorporates a piece of classical or contemporary visual art to communicate the central theme.

Each message uses a consistent format based on the following components:

PASSAGE: Each sermon is based on a specific scripture text, which is listed for reference.

PURPOSE: Each message's central theme is summarized in one simple statement.

PREPARATION: A complete bibliographical entry is given for the art selection featured in each sermon. Pictures of these works, cross-referenced in the back of this book, may be located in the following volumes:

- *Imaging the Word—An Arts and Lectionary Resource, Volume 1.* Kenneth T. Lawrence, Editor, with Jann Cather Weaver and Roger Wedell (Cleveland: United Church Press, 1994).
- *Imaging the Word—An Arts and Lectionary Resource, Volume 2.* Susan A. Blain, Editor, with Sharon Iverson Gouwens, Catherine O'Callaghan, and Grant Spradling (Cleveland: United Church Press, 1995).
- *Imaging the Word—An Arts and Lectionary Resource, Volume 3.* Susan A.Blain, Editor, with Sharon Iverson Gouwens, Catherine O'Callaghan, and Grant Spradling (Cleveland: United Church Press, 1996).

In addition, the featured art works may be found as illustrations in books, postcards, and prints in art museums and shops, and images on the Internet.

A suggestion for a teaching tool for each sermon is provided and, if needed, instructions are outlined for making or using the object.

PRESENTATION: A complete script for an interactive dialogue with the children is offered.

PRAYER: A brief prayer, suitable for repetition by the children, is given as a summary statement of the message.

Although the thirty sermons are listed by title in the contents at the beginning of the book, a significant component of this collection is the resource section at the end, which cross-references all entries by art selections—artists and titles, scripture passages, and teaching tools.

Why is this book needed?

This book—a ready-to-use collection of messages to help children explore various aspects of the church year—is unique. Since these special days are celebrated on an annual basis, church leaders must continue to find fresh approaches to familiar stories and themes. This material provides an opportunity for teachers, pastors, and parents to expand their available resources. Although there are books of children's sermons that address the seasons, there is nothing that connects the more tangible world of visual art with the intangible world of liturgy and cycles. This resource provides an extremely helpful reference allowing readers to find ways to make connections between the common events of life and the relevance of the church's message. The use of tangible teaching tools and visual works of art also allows children to review and make meaning from the pictures, as well as facilitating their intellectual growth from abstract to concrete thinking.

Who will use this book?

This book will be used in congregations by clergypersons, Christian education directors, Sunday school teachers, children's church coordinators, mid-week programmers, and special project leaders; in parochial schools by administrators and teachers; and in homes by parents and grandparents.

Messages are designed for children in kindergarten through grade five but are adaptable for boys and girls in preschool and young people in middle grades. They will also be appreciated by adults of all ages and appropriate for intergenerational audiences.

How will this book be most helpful?

In congregations, this collection will be used as children's sermons in worship, homilies in children's church, messages in Sunday school classes, reflections in mid-week ministries, meditations in youth groups, and devotions at church camp. They will also be useful as lessons in confirmation classes and religious education programs. In Christian schools, they will be used in chapel services and classroom talks. In families, they will be helpful as a focus for mealtime devotions, faith formation, and bedtime stories.

Introduction

Show Me a Picture: 30 Children's Sermons Using Visual Art is a collection designed to help church leaders and worshippers of all ages find ways to experience the Bible and the church year through visual art. In each message, the presenter uses a teaching tool to interrelate the message found in scripture, the focus of the church season, and an interpretation based on a work of art. As a part of the suggested script, the leader is prompted to engage the participants in viewing and interpreting the selected artwork.

The first prompted question is "What do you notice about this artwork?" In approaching a discussion of art, it is important to first take time to objectively observe what each viewer notices in the composition. This first step is not interpreting the content, but simply recognizing what is there. The leader should guide the participants to name or list what they see. The following categories provide possible prompts to encourage children's responses:

CONTENT: What is the subject of this painting? What objects or people do you see?

FOREGROUND/BACKGROUND/FOCAL POINT: What is closest to the viewer? What is farther away? What draws the eye as the focal point or most important point in the composition?

COLOR: What colors are used? What colors stand out?

LIGHT/SHADOW: Where is the source of light? What is in shadow?

TECHNIQUE: What pattern, texture, or line is repeated?

STYLE: Is the subject realistic or abstract? A clear depiction or an impression?

After the observers gather data about the artwork so that they have looked closely at the details and structure of the composition, then they are ready to begin to hypothesize about making personal meaning based on what they have seen. The next prompt in the dialogue is "Invite or encourage responses to the art." Keep the responses brief by asking questions as needed to guide the children's thinking, such as:

- What story or feeling does this artwork remind you of?
- What is the point of view in this picture? Where is the viewer in relation to this scene?
- Do any of the images remind you of something else? Are any images symbolic of another story or place or time?

Based on these prompts and their guiding questions, the following is an example using the painting *Christ Among the Children*, 1910, by Emil Nolde depicting the scene recorded in Mark 9:35–37. (The Museum of Modern Art, New York; *Imaging the Word—An Arts and Lectionary Resource*, Volume 1, 20, 31; Poster Set One.) In this painting, the artist uses bold strokes, minimal details, and vibrant colors to express his feelings. To help children respond to this artwork, we might begin by asking questions. Using the Nolde painting as an example, leaders might guide participants to respond in the following ways:

- What do you notice about this artwork?
- What do you see in this painting? (*Responses might include: lots of smiling children, mothers holding babies, a man with his back to us, other men standing in the dark to the left.*)
- You said the men were standing in the dark; where are the children standing? (*The children are painted in bright yellows and red. They seem to be standing in the light.*)
- Does this seem like a detailed photograph or more like an imagined scene? (*This is a picture drawn from the artist's imagination.*)

Invite or encourage responses to the art, such as: What does this imagined scene remind you of? Does it tell a story? (*It's someone's daddy who is hugging them because he's been away for a long time.*) That's a good suggestion. It does look like the man hugging the children is very glad to see them; and they look happy to see him! Is there someone in church we talk about who taught adults to be like little children? (*Jesus!*) Yes! What if I told you that the painter of this picture, Emil Nolde, loved to paint the stories from the Bible that he remembered from his childhood. *(That would explain why the painting looks like an imagined picture.)*

As we view this painting, where does the artist have the viewer stand? *(We are facing the children with Jesus.)* Right! The artist invites us to welcome the children and see their smiling faces just as Jesus does. Who might these people be who are standing in the shadow on the left of Jesus? *(People who don't seem to like the children like Jesus does.)* Jesus had to teach his disciples that they needed to become like little children if they were going to be his followers. I think that means we have to learn to love and trust Jesus just like the children in this painting.

This is just one example of the way to keep the focus on the artwork and allow children to bring and make their own meaning in response to what they see. Children's responses will certainly vary and may not be what adults expect at all. However, all responses should be valued and their participation affirmed. Leaders can always say, "I never thought of it that way before!" and learn from the experience.

1
First Sunday
in Advent: Keep Awake
Girl Standing at the Window
by Salvador Dali

PASSAGE: Mark 13:35–37

PURPOSE: Like the girl watching at the window, during Advent the church keeps awake and waits for the coming of Christ.

PREPARATION: Art selection
Girl Standing at the Window, 1925
Museo d'Arts Contemporanea, Madrid, Spain; *Imaging the Word—An Arts and Lectionary Resource, Volume 3*, 19, 78, 83.
The oil painting *Girl Standing at the Window* features an open window framing the figure of a young woman who looks out in anticipation of something yet unseen in the blue vista of sea and sky.

The artist, Salvador Dali (1904–89), was a surrealist painter, writer, and filmmaker known for the dream-like quality of his "inner landscapes."

TEACHING TOOL: Alarm clock

PRESENTATION:
Do you ever watch the clock? (*Hold up a large alarm clock.*) Sometimes? How quickly does time pass when we watch the clock? Not very fast, right? And yet when this alarm clock rings in the morning to wake me up, I feel like time has passed very quickly! On this first Sunday in Advent we are beginning to "watch the clock."

We have four Sundays until we reach an important day. Do you know what day that might be? (*Wait for someone to say, "Christmas!"*)

Yes! Advent is the time of preparing for the joy of the Christmas season. We wait for the rebirth of Jesus in our hearts, just as he was born in Bethlehem long ago. As a church we also wait for Jesus to return to earth to bring God's promised reign of peace. We have been watching and waiting for that day for over two thousand years now. Jesus did not tell his disciples at what hour he would return. He simply said we should "keep awake!" As we begin Advent, the alarm clock can remind us of Jesus' words and what we are to do during this season of preparation.

Another way to picture the message of Advent is through art. One painting in particular done by Salvador Dali, the famous Spanish artist, helps us think about what waiting for Jesus is like. (*If possible, hold up or display a print of* GIRL STANDING AT THE WINDOW). What do you notice about this painting? (*Invite and encourage responses to the art.*) I can imagine that this scene is early in the morning, just as dawn has awakened our friend in the painting, and she is looking out upon the horizon of the sea and the sky with hope. I think that is what Jesus asks the church to do during Advent—to "keep awake!"—to wait for the message of Christmas to return to us with all of its power, and to keep expecting the day when God's peace will dawn for the waiting world. Looking out at God's world with hope, like the girl standing at the window, is a much better way to wait during Advent than to just watch the clock.

PRAYER:
Dear God, thank you for the coming joy of Christmas. Help us to use this time in Advent to open the window of hope. Amen.

2

Second Sunday in Advent: Prepare

Sermon of St. John the Baptist
by Franz Pourbus the Elder

PASSAGE: Luke 3:2b–4 [1–6]

PURPOSE: Like John's words in the wilderness challenged his hearers, Advent challenges us to prepare the way for God to enter our lives through repentance and forgiveness.

PREPARATION: Art selection
Sermon of St. John the Baptist, 1569; *Musee des Beaux-Arts*, Valenciennes, France. *Imaging the Word—An Arts and Lectionary Resource, Volume 1*, 81.
The oil painting *Sermon of St. John the Baptist* depicts in a rich range of blended colors the wide range of people who responded to John's preaching.

Franz Pourbus the Elder (1545–81) was a Flemish artist known for his fine portraits.

TEACHING TOOL: Travel kit

PRESENTATION:
How long does it take you to get ready in the morning? A long time? I brought my travel kit so we can see if we all do the same kinds of things to get ready every day. (*Open the travel kit and take out related items as discussion warrants. Allow the participants to suggest some items they use.*) Do you brush your teeth? Wash your face? Comb your hair? Wow! We do a lot of the same things to get ready, don't we? Do you suppose people have always had to clean up a bit in the

morning to get ready to meet the day? I think so!

On this second Sunday in Advent, we recognize that we need to get ready for the special day that is coming. What special day is that? Oh, yes, Christmas! We know a lot about preparing for baking cookies, decorating our homes, and giving presents. However, that is not the only kind of preparing we need to do. What else might we need to do to get ready for Christmas? (*Welcome ideas.*) We prepare in lots of ways, but our scripture lesson reminds us of the words that John the Baptist used to help people get ready for the coming Messiah. John said, "Repent!" and "Prepare the way of the Lord!" That means we need to get ready on the inside—asking God's forgiveness and receiving God's cleansing within our hearts. Have people always needed this kind of "getting ready" just like they need to wash their faces, brush their teeth, and comb their hair? Yes!

We can understand more about John's message to people by looking at a famous painting. (*Hold up or display a print of* Sermon of St. John the Baptist.) What do you notice about this painting? (*Invite and encourage responses to the art.*) This work is titled *Sermon of St. John the Baptist*, and it was painted by the Flemish artist Franz Pourbus the Elder in the late 1500s. All of these different people suggest that there were many varieties of folks who came to listen to John's message. How many of them needed to prepare their hearts for God? How many of them would have needed to wash their faces, brush their teeth, or comb their hair? All of them? Yes! Just like you and me! Although people are different in many ways, and even though the way we dress changes over time, people still need to listen to John's sermon. We need to use our time in Advent to seek God's forgiveness and to cleanse our hearts to be ready to receive the coming Christ. Then we'll be ready to continue our journey to Bethlehem, travel bag and all.

PRAYER:
Dear God, thank you for the reminder that we need to get ready for Christmas. Help us to accept your gift of forgiveness as we prepare our hearts for Jesus' birth. Amen.

3
Third Sunday
in Advent: Spring Up
Red Amaryllis with Blue Background
by Piet Mondrian

PASSAGE: Isaiah 61:11

PURPOSE: Like the flowers that spring quickly from the ground, God's righteousness will be made known to all nations through the gift of the Christ Child.

PREPARATION: Art selection
Red Amaryllis with Blue Background, ca. 1907; the Museum of Modern Art, New York. *Imaging the Word—An Arts and Lectionary Resource, Volume 3*, 91.
The watercolor on paper *Red Amaryllis with Blue Background* depicts the tall stem and flower of the bulb plant called amaryllis, often associated with the holiday season.

Piet Mondrian (1872–1944) was a Dutch painter known for his abstract, geometric paintings and for contributing to the movement in art known as Neoplasticism.

TEACHING TOOL: amaryllis bulb and amaryllis flower

PRESENTATION:

Can you tell what this is going to be? (*Allow the participants to examine the Amaryllis bulb and discuss what they know about flowers that grow from bulbs.*) We really can't tell from the outside what kind of flower this is going to be, but if we have seen flower bulbs like this before we have a pretty good idea. A flower bulb is sort of like a promise, isn't it? The flower isn't here yet, but we know it's coming!

And that is like the scripture passage we read from Isaiah 61:4, telling us that God's gift of righteousness will "spring up" just like the earth sends forth shoots from the garden. The promise that Isaiah spoke of was the Messiah, God's anointed one, the righteous one of Israel, the One we know today as Jesus. The people who first heard Isaiah's words trusted that what Isaiah said about God would come true—they knew that God's promises were like flower bulbs. You might not see the flowers yet, but they were on the way!

This kind of bulb is actually an amaryllis. Have you ever grown an amaryllis at Christmas time? Because they grow quickly and are bright red in color, the amaryllis is often a favorite holiday flower and gift. Their beauty is a surprise after the long slow growth of the stem. The Dutch artist Piet Mondrian painted the bold colors and striking shape of the amaryllis in his watercolor called *Red Amaryllis with Blue Background. (Hold up or display a print of* RED AMARYLLIS WITH BLUE BACKGROUND.*)* What do you notice about this painting? *(Invite and encourage responses to the art.)* The tall flowers are beautiful. The painting is lovely. Mondrian creates a contrast of blue so that the red amaryllis seems to stand out even more. Viewing and appreciating the amaryllis in the painting is similar to hearing people tell us about God's gift of Jesus at Christmas. We can appreciate the story and understand something of God's amazing love—just like we can appreciate the beauty of the painted flower even if we've never seen it. However . . . this is even better! *(Display the blooming amaryllis plant.)*

Christmas can be just like the difference between the picture of the flower and the actual flower. As we prepare in Advent for the coming celebration, we can hear the stories of Jesus' birth and remember the importance of God's gift of a Savior. But on Christmas if we invite Jesus into our lives to be re-born in us, we can truly experience the promise of God springing up in our hearts. Then we can enjoy even more the words of Isaiah the prophet, just like we can enjoy Mondrian's painting even more after we have experienced the actual flower. How do you get an amaryllis to open by Christmas? You have to plant it early and let it grow! That's what we are doing in Advent by listening to the prophecy of Isaiah. By Christmas Sunday, we'll be ready to burst into bloom!

PRAYER:

Dear God, thank you for the promise you gave so long ago that you would send someone to save us. Help us to prepare our hearts for the beauty of Christmas when your promise is fulfilled anew. Amen.

4

Fourth Sunday in Advent: Embrace
The Meeting of the Virgin and Elizabeth by Giotto di Bondone

PASSAGE: Luke 1:39–42 [39–55]

PURPOSE: Like the joy Elizabeth knew in Mary's presence, we can sense the importance and the excitement as Christ's birth draws near.

PREPARATION: Art selection
The Meeting of the Virgin and Elizabeth, after 1306; *la capella degli Scrovegni* (Arena Chapel), Padua, Italy. *Imaging the Word—An Arts and Lectionary Resource, Volume 1*, 89.
The fresco *The Meeting of the Virgin and Elizabeth* captures the moment when Elizabeth embraces Mary, each praising God for the wonder of what was happening to them.

Giotto de Bondone (1267–1337) was a Florentine painter and architect whose genius helped inspire advances in art in the Italian Renaissance.

TEACHING TOOL: Trowel

PRESENTATION:
I have been getting supplies together in order to try my hand at being an artist. Can you guess what important tool a painter needs? (*Someone will likely say, "a brush."*) Painters do need a brush, but the kind of painting I'm thinking of learning to do requires me to use

another kind of tool first. Not a pencil, not paper—in fact this kind of painting isn't done on paper or canvas. The type of painting I want to do is called a fresco. And, to paint a fresco, what I need first is a trowel! (*Hold up a small trowel.*) A fresco is the art of painting with pigment that is applied to wet plaster. So the first step is applying the plaster with a trowel and then painting the scene while the plaster is still wet. It is challenging because there is no way to paint over or correct a fresco since the paint and the plaster bond together completely to form a new material. Fresco is an old art form, and the color and artistry of the fresco endures through time. That reminds me of the Christmas story. Jesus came to earth to be God in human form—God's spirit and human experience merged in history to form something entirely new, something that has stood the test of time.

One of the famous Italian painters known for the beautiful frescoes he created was Giotto di Bondone. In the Arena Chapel in Padua, Italy, you can still see the frescoes he painted in the 1300s. He had to work slowly because he could only paint a small section at a time working in wet plaster. One fresco Giotto painted helps us celebrate this fourth Sunday in Advent because it depicts the scene in which Mary comes to see her cousin Elizabeth. (*Hold up or display a print of* THE MEETING OF THE VIRGIN AND ELIZABETH.) What do you notice about this artwork? (*Invite and encourage responses to the art.*) Do they look excited to see each other? Maybe you can tell as they embrace that Elizabeth's baby, still in her body, leaps in excitement to be so near to God's son, the baby that Mary is carrying. This fresco would have taken a long time for Giotto to create, but the painting is famous because of how real and human Elizabeth and Mary appear and how tenderly the artist captures the moment of their joy.

As we come upon Christmas, we recognize that our excitement becomes greater and greater. Christmas challenges us, however, not just to be excited about what we can get. Instead, like Mary and Elizabeth, we are called to be excited about what we have to share with the world—the birth of a Savior who can change darkness to light and despair to hope. Maybe we will never paint a beautiful fresco like Giotto. But we can prepare ourselves to receive God's perfect gift at Christmas. We can prepare our hearts to embrace God's presence as an artist prepares the plaster to receive the paint. God's Holy Spirit can add the pigment, or color, of love. And our lives can become an enduring work of art that helps others to see that Jesus lives in us!

PRAYER:
Dear God, thank you for offering to come to dwell on earth with us. Help us to embrace your love with our whole hearts. Amen.

5
Christmas: Wonder ♪

Angels Appearing Before the Shepherds
by Henry Ossawa Tanner

PASSAGE: Luke 2:13–14 [1–20]

PURPOSE: Like the shepherds who stood in awe of the angel's message, we celebrate the wonder of God's great gift to the world.

PREPARATION: Art selection
Angels Appearing Before the Shepherds, 1910; National Museum of American Art, Smithsonian Institution, Washington, D.C. *Imaging the Word—An Arts and Lectionary Resource, Volume 1*, 98, 99; Poster Set One.

An oil on canvas, *Angels Appearing Before the Shepherds* invites the viewer to acknowledge that the angels' message is to the entire world. The shepherds in the right foreground appear as a small part of God's creation, while the horizon signifies that the good news is for all the earth.

Henry Ossawa Tanner (1859–1937), son of an African American minister, was a realist painter known for his naturalistic and religious paintings.

TEACHING TOOL: Music box mechanism

PRESENTATION:
Can you hear the music? (*Hold up the mechanism for a music box and turn the crank.*) I know it sounds faint. This is the mechanical part of a music box, but the box part is missing. As I turn the crank, watch the moving parts that create the sound vibrations. (*Allow the participants to observe the movement.*) Do you wonder why the sound

is so hard to hear? Let me show you something. (*Hold the movement against a large wooden surface such as a communion table, pulpit, or steps.*) Wow! That really makes a difference, doesn't it? You see, the wood serves as a "sounding board." The vibrations of the metal are amplified by the wood, which makes the sound seem larger and helps it carry farther. This simple music box can teach us something about Christmas, too.

God's love is like the sound from the music box. The music of God's love is always playing, but sometimes people don't listen carefully enough to hear God's message. To help human beings hear more clearly, God sent Jesus to earth. Jesus is like God's "sounding board." Given human form, the message of God's love seems closer; the sound seems louder. We can experience the wonder of God's love for all the world as we hear the story of Jesus' birth and as we experience the joyful sound of the angel chorus proclaiming the glory of God.

Most artists who have painted the story of the angels appearing to the shepherds have emphasized the shepherds or the angels. But an African American artist, Henry Ossawa Tanner, who lived at the turn of the twentieth century, emphasized nature and the grandeur of creation instead. (*Hold up or display a print of* ANGELS APPEARING BEFORE THE SHEPHERDS.) What do you notice about this picture? (*Allow the participants to respond to the art.*) In Tanner's painting, the shepherds are only a small part of God's creation. He seems to help us understand that the whole earth rejoiced to hear the good news. Maybe when we realize that we—as small as we are—are invited to join all of creation in the praise of God's glory, then we, too, become part of God's sounding board. We help amplify the joyful message of God's love for the world. (*Demonstrate again the effect of the "sounding board."*)

PRAYER:
Dear God, thank you for sending Jesus to help us hear your loving message. We want to be your sounding boards to share the good news with all the world. Amen.

6
Christmas: Embody
Hopi Virgin Mother and Child
by John Giuliani

PASSAGE: John 1:16

PURPOSE: Like an egg symbolizes birth and new life, our contemplation of the Madonna and Child leads us to new understandings of the symbols of Christmas.

PREPARATION: Art selection
Hopi Virgin Mother and Child, 1992; Burlington, VT: Bridge Building Images. *Imaging the Word—An Arts and Lectionary Resource, Volume 3*, 109.
Hopi Virgin Mother and Child is an egg tempera representation of an icon using a Native American perspective.

John Giuliani (1933–) is a Roman Catholic priest trained in the classical technique of Byzantine icon painting. His study of traditional spiritual and artistic disciplines led him to pursue the use of Native American Indian images to represent "the holy."

TEACHING TOOL: Egg

PRESENTATION:
What does this image symbolize for you? (*Hold up an egg, narrow end up.*) We usually associate eggs with Easter rather than Christmas, but eggs are a symbol for birth. So it seems natural to connect this shape with the Christmas story, too. (*Guide the respondents to understand that symbols remind us of other ideas, like an egg can represent breakfast or chickens, but also new beginnings or hope.*)

A Roman Catholic priest named John Giuliani studied a type of religious painting called icons. An icon is an artist's attempt to put a face on God. When we gaze at the artists' painted icons, we find many ways to think about God and what God's holiness means to us on earth. An icon isn't simply meant to be explained, but we are to spend our lives contemplating the meanings about God that we can bring to the picture. Many artists have painted icons of Mary and Jesus. Here is an icon that John Giuliani painted called *Hopi Virgin Mother and Child*. (*Hold up or display a print of* HOPI VIRGIN MOTHER AND CHILD.) What do you notice about this painting? (*Invite or encourage responses to the art.*) Hopi people are Native Americans, so John Giuliani is asking us to look for God's presence through the faces of people who were the original settlers of North America. Do you notice the egg shape of the Madonna's image? Giuliani gives us many ideas to consider about God in this icon.

At Christmas, we can become accustomed to our usual ideas about baby Jesus in a manger and the pictures we carry in our minds of what Christmas means. A painting such as *Hopi Virgin Mother and Child* challenges us to be aware of God's presence in the faces all around us. We can also find new symbols—such as an egg—to remind us that Jesus' birth is the message of hope for all people. Amazingly, John Giuliani created this beautiful icon from egg tempura, a kind of paint made from eggs. This icon, then, can even represent a fuller meaning of Christmas. Like the egg is both the image and the paint in this icon, Jesus is both the image of God and also the One who offered his life for us. We can spend a lifetime contemplating the amazing possibilities found in such a gift of love.

PRAYER:
Dear God, thank you for giving us ways to understand more about you. As we celebrate Jesus' birth this Christmas, help us to find new visions of how your love takes shape in our lives. Amen.

7
Christmas: Recognize
Presentation of Christ in the Temple
by Rembrandt Harmensz van Rijn

PASSAGE: Luke 2:26, 36a, 38

PURPOSE: As we celebrate the birth of the Christ Child, we recognize God's gift of the promised Messiah, just as we might recognize the work of an artist by the painting's brushstrokes.

PREPARATION: Art selection
Presentation of Christ in the Temple, ca. 1627–28; *Kunsthalle*, Hamburg, Germany. *Imaging the Word—An Arts and Lectionary Resource, Volume 3*, 103.
An oil on panel, *Presentation of Christ in the Temple*, portrays the interplay of the biblical characters who first understood Jesus to be God's Messiah.

Rembrandt Harmensz van Rijn (1606–69) was a Dutch Baroque painter who specialized in portraits and history painting. Rembrandt ranks as one of the greatest painters in the history of Western art.

TEACHING TOOL: Magnifying glass

PRESENTATION:
Have you ever heard of an artist named Rembrandt? (*Allow the participants to share what they know.*) We may not know a lot about art, but most people have heard of the master painter Rembrandt. As an artist he created more than six hundred paintings, so sometimes people discover an old painting and have it appraised, hoping that an expert might say, "Yes, you have a Rembrandt here!" That would be an amazing and valuable discovery! Someone would have to be a

student of art and look at the painting very carefully to determine if it were really an original Rembrandt. (*Hold up the magnifying glass.*) The expert would look at the style of the painting, the colors and types of oils, but most of all he or she would study the brushstrokes and the technique of the artist. (*Allow the participants to examine the print with the magnifying glass.*) I expect that if you studied a lot of Rembrandt's paintings, you would be able to recognize Rembrandt's work easily. You would be an expert!

Can we also learn to recognize God's artistry? Of course, we can! In fact, at Christmas we often read the story of two experts who recognized God's handiwork when Mary and Joseph first brought Jesus to the temple in Jerusalem. Simeon was an old man who was waiting for God to reveal to him the coming Messiah, the Anointed One who would save the world. Anna was an old woman who lived in the temple, praising God and praying night and day. Each of them immediately recognized that Jesus was the One whom God had sent to earth, the promised Messiah.

In this painting of Rembrandt's called *Presentation of Christ in the Temple*, we see the story of this moment of recognition. (*Hold up or display a print of* PRESENTATION OF CHRIST IN THE TEMPLE.) What do you notice about this painting? (*Invite or encourage responses to the art.*) Rembrandt was famous for his ability to capture facial expression and to portray characters who catch the viewer's imagination. In Rembrandt's portrayal of Anna and Simeon we see the delight of their discovery of the Christ Child. Rembrandt not only comprehended color and design; he also understood the message of Christmas. He painted two characters who had lived in such close study and relationship with God that they could easily recognize God's handiwork—Jesus the Messiah, God's signature of love.

PRAYER:
Dear God, thank you for sending Jesus, the Messiah. Help us to become experts on the love he came to share with the world. Amen.

8

Epiphany—
Magi: Reveal
The Adoration of the Magi
by Peter Paul Rubens

PASSAGE: Matthew 2:11-12 [1-12]

PURPOSE: God's gift of love in Christ is revealed to the world through the visit of the Magi, whose greatest gift to us was their journey to adore the newborn King.

PREPARATION: Art selection
The Adoration of the Magi, 1624; *Musees Royaux des Beaux Arts*, Antwerp, Belgium. *Imaging the Word—An Arts and Lectionary Resource, Volume 1*, 109, 110.
The Adoration of the Magi, oil on panel, portrays the visit of the Magi to the manger in Bethlehem with all of the attendant confusion and accompanying entourage in the imagined scene.

Peter Paul Rubens (1577–1640) was a Flemish Baroque era painter, often called the Prince of Baroque painters. He united Flemish and Italian art with his inventive style, influencing a great number of other artists. His paintings number more than three thousand and are scattered in museums throughout the world.

TEACHING TOOL: Gift box containing figures of three Wise Men

PRESENTATION:
Everyone loves presents, right? (*Hold up the unopened gift box.*) Do you know that most of the world exchanges gifts, not on December 25, but on January 6, the twelfth day after Christmas known as Epiphany? Epiphany means "revelation" and is the story of the

presentation of the very first Christmas gifts. Do you know what those were? There were three of them! *(Prompt the listeners to respond with the three gifts mentioned in Matthew 2:11-12.)* Yes, the visitors to Bethlehem that we often call "the Magi" or "the Wise Men," brought gold, frankincense, and myrrh. Of course, there had been an even more important gift to them already—the gift of Jesus to the world. On Epiphany, the traditional day for remembering the visit of the Magi, we celebrate that God's welcoming love was revealed as a gift to all people—even those who were different and from far away like those "kings from the East."

That visit must have created quite a scene! Many artists have tried to represent this important moment, this "epiphany" to the world. *(Hold up or display a print of* THE ADORATION OF THE MAGI.) What do you notice about this painting? *(Invite or encourage responses to the art.)* This famous painting by Peter Paul Rubens tells a story with lots of characters and details. Some are almost funny. However, we can still see their gifts fit for a king, and we can understand the importance of this moment as the Magi do, even in the middle of the noisy, crowded stable. God is welcoming and accepting them no matter where they came from or how they look or dress.

There is one more gift in this scene that Rubens helps us to understand. *(Open the gift box to reveal the figures.)* There is a gift to us from the Magi as well. Those who came from afar to find the Christ Child make us remember how important it is to seek for God's presence. We can experience God's revelation, but we must be willing to make the effort to search for God in unlikely places. We must be willing to give the gift of ourselves and our time, just like those pictured by Rubens in his painting. We might be surprised by what we find at the end of our journey, but God promises the revelation will be worth the trip!

PRAYER:
Dear God, thank you for sharing the gift of Jesus with everyone. We are ready to take the journey of faith, to bring you the best gift of all—ourselves. Amen.

9
Epiphany—Baptism: Center
The Baptism of Jesus Christ by Pheoris West

PASSAGE: Luke 3:21-22 [15-17, 21-22]

PURPOSE: At Epiphany we celebrate the baptism of Jesus, recognizing the challenge to center our lives on God.

PREPARATION: Art selection
The Baptism of Jesus Christ, 1993; Artist's Collection, Columbus, Ohio. *Imaging the Word—An Arts and Lectionary Resource, Volume 1*, 113; Poster Set One.
The contemporary acrylic painting of *The Baptism of Jesus Christ* depicts with color and symbolic images an active figure of Jesus standing in the Jordan River and receiving the Holy Spirit.

Pheoris West (1950–) is an art professor at the Ohio State University and a contemporary African American symbolist painter who uses the rich colors, forms, and figures of African origin to interpret sometimes life-sized figures.

TEACHING TOOL: Drawing compass and T-square

PRESENTATION:
What kind of tools do artists use to create a picture? (*Allow responses. Most likely responders will think of brushes and paints.*) Yes, those are all good suggestions. Do you suppose artists ever use tools like these? (*Hold up the drawing compass and T-square and briefly explain their names and uses.*) Sometimes artists might use these—especially

if the artist is laying out the first shapes that suggest the images he or she is planning to represent. Circles and angles are geometric shapes that we often find in contemporary paintings. One contemporary painter known for his use of color and forms is Pheoris West, an African American artist and associate professor of art at the Ohio State University. Here is an example of West's rich style in this painting called *The Baptism of Jesus Christ*. *(Hold up or display a print of* THE BAPTISM OF JESUS CHRIST.*)* What do you notice about this painting? *(Invite and encourage responses to the art.)*

Pheoris West has created a striking figure of Christ, maybe surprising us with a dark-skinned Jesus. Notice how he suggests the movement of Jesus' head, turning to the center to look directly at the one viewing the painting. If you look carefully, you will also see that there is another figure in the painting, a very angular representation of John the Baptist. *(Point out the profile and arm in the far right and bottom section of the painting.)* In contrast to the straight lines are the circles in the water, the circle of the sun, and the sense of the Spirit's movement around the body of Jesus. Pheoris West seems to suggest to us a Jesus who has found the center of God's purpose for his life, and—now baptized—is facing forward, centered on his mission.

At Epiphany, we remember the message of Jesus' baptism—that God called Jesus to a special task, named Jesus as God's Chosen One, and gave Jesus the power of the Holy Spirit to accomplish God's mission on Earth. There is also a message in that story and in this painting for us. As the compass point holds firm in the center to allow the pencil to make perfect circles, as the T-square directs the trajectory of lines and angles, God forms the center and shapes the direction for our lives.

PRAYER:
Dear God, thank you for sending Jesus to show us how to live a life with you at the center. We want you to shape and direct our lives each day. Amen.

10

Epiphany— Transfiguration: Transform
The Transfiguration by Raphael

PASSAGE: Mark 9:2, 7–8

PURPOSE: When we truly recognize Christ's transcendent power, our lives find new focus.

PREPARATION: Art selection
The Transfiguration, ca. 1519–20; *Pinacoteca*, Vatican Museums, Vatican State, Italy. *Imaging the Word—An Arts and Lectionary Resource, Volume 3*, 149.
This tempera grassa on wood painting depicts the transfiguration of Christ in glory in contrast to the foreground depiction of the Apostles trying to cure the youth who was possessed.

Raphael (1483–1520), also known as Raffaello Sanzio, was an Italian High Renaissance painter.

TEACHING TOOL: Jesus optical illusion

PRESENTATION:
Have you ever seen this optical illusion before? (*Hold up or point to the optical illusion of the word JESUS.*) If you have, perhaps you know how to look at this image. If you have not seen it before, you may be confused. (*Invite those who have not seen it before to describe what they see.*) When you first look at these shapes, they don't seem to mean anything. However, if you look at the space inside the shapes rather

than the shapes themselves, you may begin to see some familiar letters. *(Allow some time for those who are attempting to decode the illusion to try to see the word. Give hints by pointing out the "J" if necessary.)* Suddenly, the word will take shape and you'll be able to read it. *(Allow someone who can see the word to share that the shapes form the word "Jesus.")* This is called an "optical illusion," meaning that the image plays a trick on your eyes. Even though you can see the sign, you can't read it because your eyes are focusing on the wrong shapes. Once you understand what you are seeing, it becomes easy to find the hidden meaning.

Great art is not usually an optical illusion, but sometimes we have to study a painting closely to really understand the message that the artist has included in the image. During the Renaissance, great artists were often commissioned by wealthy patrons to create a visual interpretation of a biblical story. One of the famous Italian Renaissance painters was named Raphael. A very wealthy and powerful man named Cardinal Medici asked Raphael—who was the chief architect on Saint Peter's Cathedral in Rome—to paint the story of Christ's transfiguration. It was the last work that Raphael ever completed, for he died shortly after painting this masterpiece. This final painting is considered his greatest. *(Hold up or display a print of* THE TRANSFIGURATION *and relate a few details about the story depicted.)* What do you notice about this painting? *(Invite and encourage responses to the art.)*

One of the interesting ideas that Raphael includes in his interpretation of this scene is that he tells two stories at once in this painting. While Jesus is being glorified on the Mount of Transfiguration, the disciples are in the valley below trying to heal a young boy who is ill. Of course, the end of this story is that Jesus returns to the valley after his mountaintop experience and completes for the disciples what they have been unable to do: he heals the child. Maybe the message is almost the same as the optical illusion we viewed earlier. The disciples did not fully understand who Jesus was. They were looking at the problem they were trying to solve, instead of keeping their eyes on Jesus. Perhaps Raphael was trying to remind us of the importance of looking to Jesus not what is going on around us, is to be the focus of our lives. Just like Jesus was transformed by God's power on the mountain, we can learn to look to Jesus and find the transforming power of God for our lives.

PRAYER:

Dear God, thank you for your transforming power. Help us to keep our focus on Jesus as we live each day in your presence. Amen.

11
Ash Wednesday: Repent

Receiving Ashes from *The Hours of the Duchess of Bourgogne*

Passage: Psalm 51:10–12

Purpose: At the beginning of Lent, we use ashes to remind us that Christ died for our sins, to remember that we must rely on God each moment of life's journey, and to mark the beginning of our preparation for Easter.

Preparation: Art selection
Receiving Ashes, ca. 1450, manuscript illumination from *The Hours of the Duchess of Bourgogne*
Musee Conde, Chantilly, France. *Imaging the Word—An Arts and Lectionary Resource, Volume 2*, 145.
In the illuminated manuscript *Receiving Ashes*, the Latin phrases are framed with vignettes symbolic of Lent: the outward acts of pruning and planting a vineyard, the inner life of nurture and care, the Christian community confessing their sins, and—ultimately—the communion of the Saints in eternity.

Artist Unknown: During the fifteenth century, nobles like the Duchess of Bourgogne commissioned local artisans to produce lavishly illuminated manuscripts of Books of Hours, or prayers, for private devotion. The city of Paris was renowned as a major center of illumination during this time period.

Teaching Tool: Hourglass

Presentation:
(Hold up the hour glass and let the sand flow through.) Do any of you use

an hourglass to tell the time at your house? *(Discuss the need for this kind of timer before the days of clocks or watches.)* Watching the sand flow through the hourglass reminds us that time is passing quickly. In the Middle Ages, people had another way of marking the hours of the day called a *Book of Hours.* These volumes were made by hand with a page for each hour of the day containing a scripture passage, poem, or inspiring message. Readers could use the book to help them pray and be close to God during that hour of the day. Each page would be "illuminated," meaning that an artist would have painted a picture to give visual support to the words and message the page contained. Here is an illuminated manuscript called *Receiving Ashes* from a medieval *Book of Hours. (Hold up or display a print of the illuminated manuscript,* Receiving Ashes.*)* What do you notice about this artwork? *(Invite and encourage responses to the art.)* This page seems to show a special day from the church year called Ash Wednesday.

In the lower right corner a priest is placing ashes on the heads of people who are bowed in prayer. This special service occurs on the first day of the church season called Lent, a time of preparing for Easter. The ashes remind us that Jesus died for our sins. They also remind us that if we are to experience the joy of Easter, then we must experience the grief of Jesus' death. We want to tell God that we are sorry Jesus had to die for us to know how much God wants to forgive us. Telling God how sorry we are and asking God to create in us a clean heart is called repentance. We repent on Ash Wednesday and receive ashes to remember the importance of the next forty days as we prepare for Easter.

All human beings have needed ways of measuring time, whether with an hourglass, a *Book of Hours,* or a digital watch. But what is important is what we do with the time we are given. Lent is a measure of time in the church when Christians think about how much we need to rely on God every moment of life. Like an hourglass comes to the end of the sand, each human life comes to an end, as well. What we understand at Easter is that Christ's victory assures us that God has a gift of eternity waiting for those who offer the moments of their lives to God's use. *(Turn the hourglass around to begin the time again.)* And, in eternity, life never ends.

PRAYER:

Dear God, create in us a clean heart so that we may know the joy of your presence and have the hope of eternity. Amen.

12
First Sunday in Lent: Know

Original Sin and Explusion from Paradise (The Fall of Man)
by Michelangelo Buonarotti

PASSAGE: Genesis 3:3–5

PURPOSE: On the first Sunday of Lent, we remember that the human temptation to play God brings sin and death.

PREPARATION: Art selection
Original Sin and Explusion from Paradise (The Fall of Man), 1509–10; Sistine Chapel, Vatican City. *Imaging the Word—An Arts and Lectionary Resource Volume 2,* 149.
This famous fresco on the ceiling of the Sistine Chapel in the Vatican depicts the yielding to temptation of Adam and Eve, representing the fall of humankind and the entrance of sin into the world. The forbidden fruit, symbolized as an apple, is boldly and greedily accepted by the first humans, as they recline in the beauty of the first paradise, Eden.

Michelangelo Buonarotti (1475–1564) was an Italian High Renaissance/Mannerist painter and sculptor, commissioned by Pope Julius II to redecorate the renovated ceiling of his private worship space in the Vatican. Michelangelo spent years painting the story of humans from creation to the last judgment on the ceiling of the Sistine Chapel.

TEACHING TOOL: Artificial apple

PRESENTATION:

M-m-m-m! Who would like a bite of my apple? (*Wait for responses.*) I don't know. I'm tempted to keep it for myself! It looks so good! Does it look tempting to you, as well? There is nothing better than a cold, crisp, ripe apple. However, I don't want to be selfish, so I guess I should share it. (*Choose an eager volunteer to receive the apple.*) Here you go! (*Wait for the volunteer to realize the apple is artificial.*) Ah! I tricked you, right? This apple is pretty to look at, but it is not really an apple, is it? It is artificial. When you thought it was real, were you tempted to take a bite? Now it doesn't seem so tempting, does it? On this first Sunday of Lent, we often think about the story in the Bible of when the first human beings, Adam and Eve, were tempted. Their story helps us understand the problem called "sin" that all human beings face. (*Briefly tell the story from Genesis of Adam and Eve's fall from grace.*)

Adam and Eve's story has been the subject for many artists, but perhaps the most famous of all is the painting from the Sistine Chapel in Rome by Michelangelo called *Original Sin and Expulsion from Paradise*. (*Hold up or display a print of* ORIGINAL SIN AND EXPULSION FROM PARADISE.) What do you notice about this artwork? (*Invite and encourage responses to the art. Be prepared to discuss the nudity. Explain that before the fall, Adam and Eve were not even aware of their nakedness and did not need to feel ashamed. God made our bodies, and we can appreciate their beauty.*) Notice that Michelangelo painted the fruit of the tree of the knowledge of good and evil as an apple. The Bible doesn't really say what the fruit was, but the sweet, red fruit of the apple has come to be the symbol of temptation. However, Adam and Eve's sin was not that they wanted to eat an apple. Their sin was in wanting to be able to judge what was good and what was evil, just like God. If we knew everything and could judge perfectly, then we wouldn't even need God. So the temptation that we call original sin is really the temptation to be God ourselves and to live by our own knowledge, not by faith.

This is the first Sunday in Lent, marking the beginning of our journey toward Easter. On this Sunday we remember that we are creatures who, like Adam and Eve, long to know and understand. As Christians, however, we recognize that we can't know everything; we can't be God. During Lent we give up our temptation to play God ourselves and seek to come to know the God who created us, the God who sent Jesus, the second Adam, to restore us to relationship with God and with one another. Lent is a time to say "no" to sin. That's really not so difficult if we remember that temptation is an illusion. It may look good, but it isn't the real thing. *(Hold up the artificial apple.)* Maybe we should make a sign to remind us of our goal in Lent: No (n-o) sin; Know (k-n-o-w) God!

PRAYER:
Dear God, Strengthen us to resist temptation and help us to remember to live by faith in you. Amen.

13
Second Sunday
in Lent: Acknowledge
Visit of Nicodemus to Christ
by John LaFarge

PASSAGE: John 3:1–3

PURPOSE: During our Lenten journey, we are challenged to acknowledge that Jesus is the One sent by God and to take this message to the world.

PREPARATION: Art selection
Visit of Nicodemus to Christ, 1880; National Museum of American Art, Smithsonian Institution, Washington, D.C. *Imaging the Word—An Arts and Lectionary Resource, Volume 2*, 155.
This oil on canvas painting represents the nighttime meeting of Nicodemus and Jesus. The elder and important personage of Nicodemus sits in light with a scroll unrolled in his lap, apparently contemplating the Holy Scriptures with Jesus, who sits quietly, slightly above and to the right of the older man.

John LaFarge (1835–1910), a noted member of the American Arts and Crafts movement, was famous in his own lifetime for exquisite murals, stained glass designs, and innovative technique.

TEACHING TOOL: Business card

PRESENTATION:
May I have your calling card please? (*Wait to see if anyone responds.*) You don't have a calling card? I'm not surprised. A calling card was an old fashioned way of telling people your name and where you came from. People "called" on—or visited—one another and left their cards as an invitation to return the visit. Today what we have left from that time of formal manners is what we call a business card

that lets folks know who we are, what we do, and how to contact us. *(Produce a business card.)* In fashionable society of the 1800s, important people always carried a printed calling card with the person's name, title, and address. In New York in the 1800s, a famous artist like John LaFarge would most definitely have had a calling card to promote his art studio. Here is one of his famous paintings, called *Visit of Nicodemus to Christ*, that was displayed in the World's Columbian Exposition of 1893. *(Hold up or display a print of VISIT OF NICODEMUS TO CHRIST.)* What do you notice about this painting? *(Invite and encourage responses to the art.)*

This painting tells the story found in the Bible in John 3. Nicodemus, an important man in Israel, wouldn't have carried a business card, but people would have recognized him by the beautiful robes he wore. That is probably why he came to visit Jesus at night. He didn't want people to know he was coming to see the young rabbi who had other important religious leaders upset. And yet Nicodemus acknowledged that Jesus had come from God. He recognized God's "calling card" of healings and wonders that Jesus had performed. Nicodemus knew that no one could do such mighty works unless he had been sent by God. In the painting, Nicodemus and Jesus seem to be discussing the Holy Scriptures. Notice the unrolled scroll resting in Nicodemus' lap. And notice the light that seems to surround Nicodemus and rest on Jesus' hands. LaFarge seems to suggest that although Nicodemus came in the dark, he had seen the light.

During Lent, we have an opportunity to acknowledge who Jesus is. Like Nicodemus, we need to recognize that only God could have sent Jesus to bring understanding, healing, and hope to the world. God's "calling cards" are all around us. We see them in the Bible, in God's love for the world, in people's working together to help others, and in worship as we sense Christ's presence. When—like Nicodemus—we find the courage to come and visit Jesus, then we take with us God's message to a hurting world. And our lives become another "calling card" of God's love.

PRAYER:
Dear God, help us to seek Jesus every day of our Lenten journey. Use our lives as one of your "calling cards" of love. Amen.

14
Third Sunday in Lent: Ask

Jesus and the Samaritan Woman
from Catacomb of via Latina, Rome, Italy

PASSAGE: John 4:7–10

PURPOSE: The Lenten message for Christians is that death is not the end of life, that we worship a God who offers us living water simply for the asking.

PREPARATION: Art selection
Jesus and the Samaritan Woman, 350–400; Catacomb of *via Latina*, Rome, Italy. *Imaging the Word—An Arts and Lectionary Resource, Volume 2*, 157.
The fresco of *Jesus and the Samaritan Woman* painted on the wall of the Catacomb of *via Latina* portrays the two standing at the well from which Jesus sought a drink.

Artist Unknown: Early Christians painted representations of biblical scenes on the walls of the catacombs during the third and fourth centuries.

TEACHING TOOL: Pulley

PRESENTATION:
Do you know what this tool is called? *(Discuss and name the pulley.)* A pulley is a way to increase the effect of force. You pull down on one side and the weight or object being lifted on the other side goes up. *(If possible, demonstrate.)* It's a simple tool, but effective. When people used to draw water from a well in Bible times, he—or, usually, she—would simply throw in a bucket made of goatskin tied to a rope, then draw the water up one small, heavy bucket at a time. It was

a difficult, daily task. But what happens to human beings without water? We die! Water is essential to life. And for the people who live in hot, dry places, water is even more precious—and even deeper in the ground.

There are many Bible stories about wells and water. One of the most famous is a story about Jesus and a woman from Samaria whom Jesus asked for a drink. Jesus was just passing through Samaria, waiting at a well for the disciples to return. The woman was surprised that Jesus even spoke to her, let alone asked her for a drink. Jesus responded that if she knew who it was who asked her, she would have asked him, and he would have given her "living water." We can interpret the idea of "living water" many ways, but, most importantly, Jesus is saying that he has the power to give us eternal life. After Jesus ascended into heaven, the first Christians met for worship in catacombs—a web of underground caverns where people were buried. In part they were hiding from authorities who opposed the church, but they also saw the importance of gathering where their loved ones were buried. As Christians, they knew that life on earth is not all there is. We worship a living God; we worship in the name of the One who offers us "living water."

One catacomb that was discovered under the city of Rome is called the Catacomb of *via Latina*. On the plastered walls of the catacombs Christians often painted scenes from the Bible, called frescoes. Guess what scene they found in the Catacomb of *via Latina*? (*Hint that they just heard this story if need be.*) Yes, here is a picture of that painting called *Jesus and the Samaritan Woman*. (*Hold up or display a print of* JESUS AND THE SAMARITAN WOMAN.) What do you notice about this painting? (*Invite and encourage responses to the art.*) For those early Christians, and for us, the symbol of the well and life-giving water is easy to interpret. Maybe there is also another symbol here. Pulling water from a deep well is hard work. A pulley would make that work much easier. However, Jesus says that he will make finding "living water" even easier—all we have to do is ask!

PRAYER:
Dear God, thank you for sending Jesus to be our "living water." Help us to remember to drink deeply at your well. Amen.

15
Fourth Sunday in Lent: Send

Altarpiece: The Life of Christ
by Keith Haring

PASSAGE: John 3:16–17

PURPOSE: On the Fourth Sunday in Lent, we remember that God sent Jesus to earth to bring the message of God's love to every human being.

PREPARATION: Art selection
Altarpiece: The Life of Christ, 1989; Grace Episcopal Cathedral, San Francisco, California. *Imaging the Word—An Arts and Lectionary Resource, Volume 3*, 172, 173.
In his work of bronze and white gold entitled *Altarpiece: The Life of Christ*, Haring conveys his interpretation of the gospel with free-form images representing a cross, a glowing heart, and a baby resting in arms with blessings flowing down equally on all humankind.

Keith Haring (1958–90) was an American artist of popular culture. His linear style used images like barking dogs, human figures, and television sets to explore social and political themes.

TEACHING TOOL: Graffiti wall

PRESENTATION:
Have you ever seen graffiti written on walls in public places? (*Hold up the graffiti wall for all to see.*) Regrettably, we probably have all witnessed walls or signs on which people have written words or drawn pictures where they weren't supposed to. That kind of graffiti is destructive and

wrong. But can there be a good kind of graffiti? (*Let the listeners speculate.*) An American artist by the name of Keith Haring became famous by painting graffiti in the subway on the black paper used to cover old advertisements. His drawings were quite simple— pyramids, flying saucers, human figures, winged creatures, television sets, animals, and babies. Soon the baby with rays all around it became his signature. (*Point to the image(s) on the graffiti wall.*) The subway riders of New York began recognizing these drawings, although they had no idea who made them. How better to get across a positive message to lots of people on a daily basis than to create a message on the walls of the subway station?

Keith Haring didn't live to be very old. He died from a disease called AIDS when he was thirty-two. But before he died, Keith's simple line drawings became symbols of American culture. His last artistic creation was a bronze and white gold altarpiece in the traditional style of Russian religious icons. It was unveiled on December 1, 1995, World AIDS Day, and is the centerpiece of the AIDS Memorial Chapel in San Francisco's Grace Episcopal Cathedral. We might think it is odd that an artist became famous because of graffiti. Or that a famous pop artist might create an altar for a church. However, art is about communicating the meaning of life. And at the heart of the meaning of life is God.

If we look at the altarpiece that Haring designed, we can see his trademark of the baby with the rays all around it. (*If possible hold up or display a print of Haring's* ALTARPIECE: THE LIFE OF CHRIST.) What else do you notice about this artwork? (*Invite and encourage responses to the art.*) Haring echoes John 3:16—"For God so loved the world that he gave his only Son." Just like Haring sent a message to ordinary people who traveled every day on the subway, God sends a message to us during Lent. Because God loves us so much, Jesus came to save us—all of us! That's a very simple message that goes straight to our hearts—just like the artwork of Keith Haring.

PRAYER:
Dear God, thank you that Jesus came to show us your great love. Help us to send your message to everyone each day. Amen.

16
Fifth Sunday in Lent: Adopt
Klageleid des Jeremias
by Marc Chagall

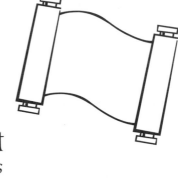

PASSAGE: Jeremiah 31:33b

PURPOSE: On the Fifth Sunday in Lent, we receive God's message as Jeremiah did that we are adopted as God's own and our hearts are sealed with the law of love.

PREPARATION: Art selection
Klageleid des Jeremias, 1956; ARS, New York. *Imaging the Word—An Arts and Lectionary Resource, Volume 3*, 177.
Chagall's original color lithograph, *Klageleid des Jeremias*, portrays the prophet as a solitary figure clutching the *Torah* as one might embrace a child, while in the distance the artist suggests faces of individuals and the skyline of a city.

Marc Chagall (1887–1985) was a Russian-born French painter and stained glass artist, recognized as one of the most significant painters and graphic artists of the twentieth century.

TEACHING TOOL: Scroll

PRESENTATION:
Do any of you write on scrolls these days? (*Hold up a scroll.*) Most of the time you probably write in notebooks. We don't use scrolls to capture our thoughts any more. Our sacred writing, the Bible, is in the form of a book today. However, in Jewish synagogues, they still use a scroll for their worship services, on which is written the *Torah*, or the first five books of the Hebrew Scriptures. The *Torah* today

looks very much as it did in the time of the prophet Jeremiah, more than 2,500 years ago. In a modern-day work of art by Marc Chagall, we can see the artist's interpretation of the prophet Jeremiah as he holds the scroll called the *Torah*. *(If possible hold up or display a print of Chagall's* KLAGELEID DES JEREMIAS.*)* What else do you notice about this work of art? *(Invite and encourage responses to the art.)*

Jeremiah seems to be holding God's law to his heart. God gave Jeremiah a vision of what God's new plan for people was to be. When God first gave Moses the law, the commandments were written in stone. Later, the words were written on scrolls. But God told Jeremiah that God's new plan was to write the words of the law on people's hearts. In other words, God's plan is for us to have the law within us, so that we know that we belong to God completely.

Maybe you thought Jeremiah looked sad in this picture. The title Marc Chagall gave this lithograph is translated from the German as "Jeremiah's Lamentations." To lament is to be sad and sorrowful. Perhaps Jeremiah is sad because, during his time, God's vision had not yet become a reality. People were living far from God's law, or they were simply keeping rules that they didn't understand. Sometimes we still feel that's true today. However, during Lent, we remember that we have greater hope because Jesus has come. We know that God's plan is now fulfilled. Through the sacrifice of Jesus we belong completely to God. Like a loving parent, God has adopted us, and we can receive God's law of love into our hearts.

PRAYER:
Dear God, thank you for the vision of hope you give to the world. Today, we open our hearts to you to receive your law of love. Amen.

17
Palm/Passion Sunday: Process
Guatemala: Procession by Betty LaDuke

PASSAGE: Mark 11:9–11a

PURPOSE: By welcoming Jesus into our lives, we discover the strength to reach out to all people in Christ's name.

PREPARATION: Art selection
Guatemala: Procession, 1978; Artist's Collection, Ashland, Oregon. *Imaging the Word—An Arts and Lectionary Resource, Volume 3*, 181; Poster Set Three.

In Betty LaDuke's acrylic painting *Guatemala: Procession*, Christ appears on a donkey surrounded by the masks worn by Guatemala's native people as they dance to honor and celebrate their indigenous roots.

Betty LaDuke (1933–) is a contemporary painter, printmaker, and author of numerous books. She paints images from her travels to a variety of cultures, emphasizing the lives of indigenous people. LaDuke lives in Ashland, Oregon, where she is professor of art at Southern Oregon State College.

TEACHING TOOL: Mask

PRESENTATION:
(Hold up a colorful mask of a person's face.) Can you recognize me behind this mask? I'm sure you can guess that it's really me, right? *(Lower the mask to reveal identity.)* How did you know who was behind the mask? *(Let the participants offer their reasoning.)* You were thinking very well! I guess I can't fool you. Today is Palm Sunday. Does anyone know what we celebrate on Palm Sunday? *(Allow volun-*

teers to retell, in general, the story of the triumphal entry, supplying clues as needed.) The crowd certainly seemed excited to see Jesus, didn't they? And yet, just a few days later, the crowd was crying for Jesus to be crucified. Do you think Jesus was fooled by their excited welcome on Palm Sunday? Do you think Jesus knew that soon many of the same people would be crying out for him to be crucified? (Remind the listeners that Jesus understood he was riding into a difficult time in his life and he knew that the crowd would be fickle.) Just like you knew who was behind this mask, Jesus knew that human beings often only want God to do their will. Jesus rode into Jerusalem determined to do God's will.

Today Christians around the world celebrate Palm Sunday in a variety of ways. We forget that other cultures and other people may have their own ways of expressing their love for God. Artist Betty LaDuke likes to travel the world and discover the traditions and images of different cultures. She weaves their stories into her paintings and captures the vivid colors of their celebrations. (If possible, hold up or display a print of GUATEMALA: PROCESSION.) What do you notice about this artwork? (Invite and encourage responses to the art.) In this acrylic painting, Guatemala: Procession, we see Jesus on a donkey just as the Bible tells the story of his triumphal entry into Jerusalem. But in LaDuke's painting, the crowd is represented by the masks the Guatemalan people wear in celebrations of their history. The people on one side of the painting are lighting candles; on the other, the woman and man are so gentle they can interact with the birds.

The painting seems to suggest a movement from the crowd and the past into the present moment of living in God's peace. That is a good message for Palm Sunday. If we are to be more than a "face in the crowd," then we must live lives of peace. We can pray. We can be gentle with God's creation. We can welcome Jesus into our lives and understand that God's will is for no one to be left out of God's parade.

PRAYER:
Dear God, thank you for the excitement and joy that we feel as we prepare for Easter. Help us to welcome Jesus into our lives so that we may know your will. Amen.

18

Holy Thursday: Reflect
Last Supper by Tintoretto (Jacopo Robusti)

PASSAGE: 1 Corinthians 11:23–26

PURPOSE: As we reflect on the mystery of God's presence within life, we remember Jesus taught us that he is with us in the simple elements of food and drink.

PREPARATION: Art selection
Last Supper, 1592–94; Church of *San Georgio Maggiore*, Venice, Italy. *Imaging the Word—An Arts and Lectionary Resource, Volume 1, 175.*

In Tintoretto's oil on canvas portrayal of the *Last Supper*, the artist captures a visionary representation of Christ and the Apostles, combining the transcendent images of angels and the mundane, shadowy work of servants with the activity of Jesus' institution of the Holy Meal.

Jacopo Robusti (1518–94), an artist who took his nickname "Tintoretto" from his father's profession of dyer (tintore), painted in the complex mannerist style of his day—emphasizing technical accuracy, but also theatrical and stylized compositions.

TEACHING TOOL: Halo

PRESENTATION:
Is my halo on straight? (*Place halo on head.*) Are the rest of you as holy as I am? I can't quite see your halos. (*Look around the crowd.*) Do you have them? I could loan you mine. (*Remove halo; allow others to try it on.*) What is a halo anyway? (*Allow participants to offer definitions.*) Often we think of a halo as the ring of light around the head of someone holy—as in paintings of Jesus or saints. I have never actually seen a halo, unless someone was wearing one like this, maybe

pretending to be an angel in a pageant. *(Replace the halo.)*

When artists of the Renaissance and later time periods wanted to suggest that a person was a saint, they painted a circle of light around that person's head. One artist of the late Renaissance was nicknamed Tintoretto. Around 1592, two years before he died, he began painting Jesus and the disciples at the Last Supper, the meal we celebrate on Holy Thursday, or Maundy Thursday, when Jesus celebrated the Passover for the last time with his disciples. *(If possible, hold up or display a print of Tintoretto's* LAST SUPPER.) What do you notice about this artwork? *(Invite and encourage responses to the art.)* Do you see the light around Jesus' head and the disciples' heads? Some suggest that the person in the red turban kneeling down—without a halo—is Judas, the disciple who betrayed Jesus. The servants serving the meal do not have halos either. Tintoretto chose to show the meal from the side of the table, revealing the whole room and all the people in it, including the spiritual world of angels.

Often when we think or talk about God's presence, we think in the style of those artists who portray the mystery of God with scenes like this. There is nothing wrong with using halos to help us understand that God's light is with us. We are called to reflect God's light to the world. We also are called to reflect in another way. On Holy Thursday we reflect, or take time to think, about what Jesus did and said that last night with his disciples. Jesus gave us the simple elements of bread and cup to use as the way to find his presence with us in life. Jesus did not give us halos to wear. He gave us food and drink—to take in for our own nourishment as we remember his sacrifice for us, but also to share with others as we offer them ways to remember how much Jesus loves each one of us. He loves us enough to offer his life in our place. That kind of love seems mysterious, but Jesus' love is very real—as real as a loaf of bread and a cup of juice or wine. We just need to see the whole picture.

PRAYER:
Dear God, thank you for the gifts that Jesus gave us to remember him. Help us to take time to reflect on Jesus' gift of the bread and cup and to share the great mystery of your love with others. Amen.

19
Good Friday: Help
Black Cross, New Mexico
by Georgia O'Keefe

PASSAGE: Psalm 22:1–2

PURPOSE: By concentrating on the cross, we find help for life in the darkest of times.

PREPARATION: Art selection
Black Cross, New Mexico, 1929; Art Institute of Chicago, Chicago, Illinois. *Imaging the Word—An Arts and Lectionary Resource, Volume 3,* 188.

In Georgia O'Keefe's oil on canvas painting of *Black Cross, New Mexico,* the artist captures the rugged beauty of the religious emblem simplified and contrasted against the evening landscape of New Mexico.

Georgia O'Keefe (1887–1986) was a pioneer of American Modernism who emphasized the essential beauty of her subjects by magnifying shapes and simplifying details.

TEACHING TOOL: Black veil

PRESENTATION:
(Put on the black veil.) Have you ever seen a mourning veil like this? *(Allow the participants to comment on their experience.)* People don't wear these as much as they used to. In the past, women always wore a black veil for a period of time after a death to indicate that they were "in mourning." *(Remove the veil.)* That meant that someone dear to them had died, and they were letting the world know of their

sadness and loss. They might dress in mourning for at least one year as they worked through their grief. Good Friday is a day set aside for mourning in the church. What happened on Good Friday? (*Let the participants review the events of Good Friday, helping them as time permits with any needed information.*) We feel sad when we think of Jesus crying for help on the cross. Even though Jesus experienced terrible pain and loneliness, he died on the cross because he loved us.

The color for Good Friday is black, the only day in the church year when we use that color. There is a famous painting by American modernist artist Georgia O'Keefe called *Black Cross, New Mexico.* (*If possible, hold up or display a print of O'Keefe's* BLACK CROSS, NEW MEXICO.) What do you notice about this artwork? (*Invite and encourage responses to the art.*) Georgia O'Keefe liked to make the details of her artwork simple, but very large, in order to help viewers stop to see the beauty they otherwise might miss. O'Keefe loved to go for walks in the evening in the southwestern desert of New Mexico. Often on her walks she would notice simple, pegged crosses that had been placed there by religious groups for others to see and be reminded to stop and think and pray. O'Keefe said that the crosses reminded her of a black veil, stretched across the beautiful landscape of New Mexico. Good Friday is also like a black veil stretched across our experience in Holy Week. (*Put the veil on again.*)

Have you ever wondered why we call the day Jesus died "Good" Friday? What can be good about someone dying? Yet, if we recognize the great sacrifice that Jesus made in giving his life, we learn just how much God loves us. The punishment for sin is death. All of us have sinned. But Jesus offered his life as our payment for the sin in our lives. When we think that Jesus took the punishment we deserved, then we recognize just how good a gift we've been given. So even though we mourn on the Friday before Easter as we remember the sacrifice Jesus made, we also celebrate. Without Christ's death, we would have no hope. Without the events on Friday, there could be no triumphant Easter Sunday. What happened to Jesus was not "good." But what happens for us as a result of his sacrifice is—we receive eternal life! When we look upon his cross and call for help, we find it! We may look through a veil on Good Friday. However, we need only mourn for three days! (*Remove the veil.*) That's good!

PRAYER:

Dear God, help us to appreciate the sacrifice that Jesus made for us. Thank you for letting us know the goodness of your love. Amen.

20
Easter: Rejoice
Christ Appearing to Mary
by Albert P. Ryder

PASSAGE: John 20:15–16 [1–18]

PURPOSE: When we experience Christ's resurrection, our hearts rejoice.

PREPARATION: Art selection
Christ Appearing to Mary, 1885; National Museum of American Art, Smithsonian Institution, Washington, D.C. *Imaging the Word—An Arts and Lectionary Resource, Volume 1*, 186.

In Ryder's oil on canvas treatment of *Christ Appearing to Mary*, the artist captures the first moments of recognition in the biblical record of Easter morning.

Albert P. Ryder (1847–1917) expresses his visionary, romantic, and highly imaginative view of life through his artwork focused on themes found in nature, literature, and religion.

TEACHING TOOL: Easter plants

PRESENTATION:
(Produce an "Easter garden" of potted plants or a spring bouquet of fresh flowers. Inhale the fragrance.) My! Doesn't that smell delightful! The fragrance of Easter flowers is one reason for rejoicing at Easter time. I wonder why we associate flowers with Easter? *(See if the listeners can offer reasons why flowers remind us of Easter.)* You have lots of good ideas why flowers are connected so strongly with Easter. Jesus rose from the dead and is alive again. Flowers remind us of new life, and hope, and beauty. All of those are good reasons for associating Easter and a spring garden. There is an Easter story that seems to take place

in a garden, too. In the Gospel of John, chapter 20, Mary Magdalene is weeping outside of Jesus' tomb. She thinks that someone has stolen the body of Jesus, and she is so sad! When someone comes up to her, who does she think the person is? A gardener! That's why many people speak of "the garden tomb." But who is the "gardener"? Right! Jesus! Can you imagine how surprised Mary is when she hears a familiar voice say her name?

An American artist named Albert P. Ryder painted a picture of that moment when Mary Magdalene realizes that the gardener is really Jesus himself, alive again. (If possible, hold up or display a print of Ryder's CHRIST APPEARING TO MARY.) What do you notice about this artwork? (Invite and encourage responses to the art.) In the painting Christ Appearing to Mary, Ryder gives us the transforming moment in Mary's life as she recognizes the One whose life had already transformed hers in so many ways. However, this transformation from death to life gives her the greatest reason to rejoice. Mary has just learned that God's love is more powerful than death, that hope triumphs over sorrow, and that eternity begins in our relationship with Jesus.

The painting of Albert P. Ryder's is based on his own personal belief in the joy of Easter sunrise. Ryder was a faithful Christian who was able to see the beauty of God's presence in nature, in literature, and in the scriptures. His painting is famous because many can appreciate the significance of a work of art. However, seeing a picture of an Easter garden is not the same as inhaling the sweet fragrance. Observing the joy on Mary's face in the painting is not the same as recognizing for ourselves that Jesus lives. Like Mary, we must experience the truth of the resurrection for ourselves. If we listen to the rhythms of the Easter hymns, recite the stories of the resurrection, and offer the prayers of our hearts, then we can experience the same moment of rejoicing—that moment when we know that our Savior lives, and he is calling to us by name.

PRAYER:
Dear God, thank you for the joy of Easter morning and the story of Mary hearing Jesus' voice. Help us to listen and hear the good news that Jesus lives today! Amen.

21
Easter: Listen
The Moorish Kitchen Maid
by Diego Rodriguez de Silva y Velazquez

PASSAGE: Luke 24:35

PURPOSE: As we listen to the Easter story, we once again learn that Christ is nearer than we realize.

PREPARATION: Art selection
The Moorish Kitchen Maid, ca. 1620; National Gallery of Ireland, Dublin. *Imaging the Word—An Arts and Lectionary Resource, Volume 2*, 190, 191; Poster Set Two.

In Velazquez's oil on canvas painting of *The Moorish Kitchen Maid*, the artist uses dark, rich colors and contrasting light to convey the common life of a young servant woman, listening intently to the resurrected Jesus at supper in the adjoining room.

Diego Rodriguez de Silva y Velazquez (1599–1660) was one of Spain's greatest painters. Influenced by the Italian Baroque artists, Velazquez is able to merge color, line, space, and light to make objects seem real and characters appear to breathe.

TEACHING TOOL: Loaf of bread in cloth-lined basket

PRESENTATION:
Guess what I have in the basket! It's one of my favorite foods! (*Let the participants offer a few guesses before revealing the bread.*) Fresh-baked bread! Yum! Bread is an important food of almost every culture. It is a basic symbol of what we need to stay alive. Bread is also a symbol of something in the church. Do you know what meaning bread has for the Christian church? (*Let a volunteer connect bread*

with the sacrament of communion and the body of Christ.) Jesus told his
followers he was the "bread of life" that came from heaven. At the
Last Supper with his disciples, Jesus broke bread with them and said,
"This is my body, broken for you." So bread is a wonderful reminder
of the mystery of God's love for us, revealed in the Easter story of
Christ's crucifixion and resurrection.

There is another Easter story that you may not know as well that
takes place after Jesus rose from the dead. On Easter morning, some
of the women came running back from the tomb claiming that an
angel told them Jesus was alive. However, some of the disciples didn't
believe that story. The claim seemed impossible, knowing what they
did about what happened to Jesus on Good Friday. They thought the
women's story was just wishful thinking. Later in Luke's Gospel, he
reports a story of two followers of Jesus who decide to leave Jerusalem
and go back to their village of Emmaus. On the way, a stranger joins
them and listens to their account of what happened to Jesus. This
stranger explains to them that scriptures predicted the Messiah
would have to suffer and die. When they arrive home, they invite the
stranger in for an evening meal. In the tradition of their culture, they
ask their guest to say the blessing over the bread. When he blesses the
bread and breaks it, suddenly they recognize that this stranger is Jesus
himself! When they return to Jerusalem, they tell the eleven disciples
what has happened, and how they recognized Jesus when he broke
the bread.

At Easter, we celebrate that Jesus came to bring the bread of life
to the world. As Christians, we work to bring bread to those who are
physically hungry, and we also share Easter's good news that feeds
those who are spiritually hungry. In his painting *The Moorish Kitchen
Maid*, Spanish painter Velázquez captures the message we find in the
story of the Emmaus road. (*If possible, hold up or display a print of
Velázquez'* The Moorish Kitchen Maid.) What do you notice about
this artwork? (*Invite and encourage responses to the art.*) The servant
girl has probably worked to provide the bread that is shared in the
meal with Jesus in the next room. But look at how intently she is
listening to what Jesus is saying. Her attitude suggests a hunger for
the good news that Jesus is alive. The painting reminds us that, as
Christians, we must share the bread of life with the world—by being

the servants who work to feed the hungry, and by listening for the voice of our resurrected Savior. In both ways, Jesus is made known to us in the breaking of the bread. *(Break the bread and share it with the participants.)*

PRAYER:

Dear God, thank you for the bread of life that sustains us. Help us to see and hear Jesus as we work together to share the good news of new life in Christ. Amen.

22

Easter: Believe
The Incredulity of St. Thomas
by Michelangelo Merisi da Caravaggio

PASSAGE: John 20:19 [19–31]

PURPOSE: By identifying with Thomas' need to see in order to believe, we can come to choose faith over doubt.

PREPARATION: Art selection
The Incredulity of St. Thomas, 1601–02; Uffizi Gallery, Florence, Italy. *Imaging the Word—An Arts and Lectionary Resource, Volume 1*, 191.

In his oil on canvas painting entitled *The Incredulity of St. Thomas*, Michelangelo Merisi da Caravaggio portrays the encounter of the doubting disciple with the risen Christ in a realistic interpretation, relying on strong natural light to heighten the drama.

Michelangelo Merisi da Caravaggio, 1573–1610, was a Baroque Italian painter noted for his realistic depiction of religious subjects and his novel use of light.

TEACHING TOOL: Litmus paper; samples of acid and base solutions such as ammonia, baking soda and water, lemon juice, and white vinegar

---

PRESENTATION:
(Set up samples of acid and base solutions for the "experiment.") Do you like to do science experiments? Science experiments help us to discover the truth about substances we find in nature. Some solutions are acids and some are bases. In order to know about the chemical make up of a solution, scientists can use a special paper called "litmus

paper" to find out whether something is acidic or alkaline. (*Hold up a piece of litmus paper.*) Let's try an experiment. (*Allow three participants to each dip a strip of litmus paper into one of the solutions. Discuss how the difference in color "proves" which one is the base.*) The study of science gives us a logical way to discover the rules that govern our world. The more we understand, the more we can solve problems and discover new possibilities to help people. To be a scientist is to search for truth and to test to see if what you think is true, really is.

Can people who need proof also be people of faith? One of the stories from the Gospel of John tells us that one of the disciples, named Thomas, wanted proof that Jesus had really risen from the dead. He had seen Jesus nailed to the cross. He had seen the spear pierce Jesus' side. He could not simply accept the other disciples' claim that they had seen Jesus. Thomas doubted the Easter story. What do you think Jesus did about that? Did he write off Thomas as a disciple because he didn't believe? (*Allow some speculation and hypothesizing about the situation.*) Jesus chose to appear to Thomas and invite him to see for himself—to touch the wounds from the nails and the wound on his side.

This dramatic moment in the Easter story has been painted many times. One of the most famous representations was depicted in the early 1600s by Michelangelo Merisi da Caravaggio, an Italian artist who tried to make his subjects appear more realistic. (*If possible, hold up or display a print of* THE INCREDULITY OF ST. THOMAS.) What do you notice about this artwork? (*Invite and encourage responses to the art.*) The comforting truth is that Jesus allowed Thomas to have the proof the doubting disciple needed in order to find faith. John records that Thomas fell to his knees at Jesus' feet and exclaimed, "My Lord and my God!" However, Jesus told Thomas that an even greater blessing belongs to those who do not see and yet believe. It is easy to believe when we have the proof. The true "litmus test" of being a Christian is choosing to live by faith.

PRAYER:
Dear God, thank you for the Easter challenge to live by faith. Help us to choose each day to follow our living Savior. Amen.

23
Ascension Day: Dance
The Ascension by Bagong Kussudiardja

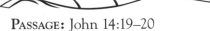

PASSAGE: John 14:19–20

PURPOSE: When we truly understand that Christ has triumphed over death, then we can live life as a victory dance.

PREPARATION: Art selection
The Ascension, 1998; in Takenaka, Masao and Ron O'Grady, The Bible Through Asian Eyes (Auckland, New Zealand: Pace Publishing in association with the Asian Christian Art Association, 1991), 165. Imaging the Word—An Arts and Lectionary Resource, Volume 2, 202.

In his depiction of The Ascension, the artist expresses the Asian imagery of the bird in flight to convey the freedom of the ascending Christ.

Indonesian artist Bagong Kussudiardja, 1928–2004, depicts Asian imagery in his paintings to convey Christian themes.

TEACHING TOOL: Feathers

PRESENTATION:
(Hold a feather in the palm and blow to make it airborne. If appropriate, have the participants keep blowing to keep the feather aloft. Then capture the feather again for a closer look.) Feathers are amazing inventions! The quill in the center is hollow so that the feather can be lightweight. Fuzzy feathers like this are called "down feathers." They serve as insulation underneath the contour feathers on the outside of a bird. Human beings have always been fascinated by the bird's

ability to fly. Birds have been symbols of freedom and hope in many cultures. In the Christian church, we use the symbol of the dove to represent the quiet presence of God that descends to us in baptism. In the Asian culture, birds are often the subjects of artwork, especially the crane, one of the largest birds that flies. In Asia, the crane is used to symbolize immortality—or eternal life.

It is not surprising, then, that an Indonesian artist named Bagong Kussudiardja combined the symbol of a bird in flight with the figure of Jesus to express the Christian understanding of Christ's ascension. *(If possible, hold up or display a print of* THE ASCENSION.*)* What do you notice about this artwork? *(Invite and encourage responses to the art.)* The figure of Jesus in the painting seems almost to be dancing, rather than flying. When Jesus returned to the eternal place where God dwells that we call heaven, he promised his disciples that he would send the Holy Spirit. He promised that because he was living they, too, would live. The way the disciples—and you and I—continue to see Jesus is through the mystery of the Holy Spirit, Christ dwelling both in God and in us.

When the Holy Spirit comes to us, we don't grow feathers. However, we do experience the joy that *The Ascension* seems to suggest. Although Jesus returned to God, we are not alone. Jesus is triumphant over sin and death. The Holy Spirit is with us. We have much to celebrate! And that good news makes us feel almost lighter than air. *(Blow the feather into the air.)*

PRAYER:
Dear God, thank you for the promise of the Holy Spirit who comes to dwell with us. Help us to celebrate the good news that Jesus gives us eternal life. Amen.

24

Pentecost: Fill
Pentecost from the *Rabbula Gospel*

PASSAGE: Acts 2:1, 4

PURPOSE: As we are filled with the Spirit, our lives proclaim the glory of God.

PREPARATION: Art selection
Pentecost from the *Rabbula Gospel*, ca. mid-sixth century; *Biblioteca Medicea Laurenziana*, Florence, Italy. *Imaging the Word—An Arts and Lectionary Resource, Volume 2*, 208, 212. Poster Set Two.

In the illuminated manuscript on parchment found in the *Rabbula Gospel*, an anonymous illustrator depicts the gift of the Holy Spirit to Mary and the apostles at Pentecost.

Anonymous Illustrator

TEACHING TOOL: Calligraphy pen and gold ink

PRESENTATION:
(If possible, fill a calligraphy pen with gold ink and demonstrate fancy writing.) We don't often use pens that have to be filled with ink in order to write. Long ago people didn't even have pens. They wrote using a quill pen made from a feather. The hollow tube in the center of the feather could be dipped in ink so that the scribe could write, using the beautiful letters we call "calligraphy." The scribes were usually religious followers who dedicated their lives to copying the stories from the Bible. There were no duplicating machines or typewriters, so all books had to be printed by hand. Not only did they write the sacred words from the scriptures, they also illustrated the pages with colorful pictures and designs that represented important

biblical moments—like scenes from the life of Jesus or stories from the early church. We call these collections of writing and pictures "illuminated manuscripts."

One very early illuminated manuscript is called the *Rabbula Gospel* because it is signed by a scribe named Rabbula. The manuscript's pages contain images of early Christian art done by anonymous artists. One illumination is simply called *Pentecost* because it represents the story of the gift of the Holy Spirit. (*If possible, hold up or display a print of* PENTECOST *from the* RABBULA GOSPEL.) What do you notice about this artwork? (*Invite and encourage responses to the art.*) This picture of the Pentecost story presents the symbols of the Holy Spirit—the descending dove and the tongues of flame—described in the second chapter of Acts. This artist also places Mary at the center of the group of apostles, suggesting her importance to the early church.

Most early illuminated manuscripts were drawn in shades of red, blue, and gold. Berries and other natural colors provided the red and blue, but the gold came from real gold! Illuminated manuscripts were treasured works of art, not only because they were time-consuming and expensive to create, but also because they contained the most valuable treasure of all—God's Word. The illuminators' pens were filled with ink made of precious gold so that they could reflect the beauty of God's light and love—just like our lives today when they are filled with the Holy Spirit.

PRAYER:
Dear God, thank you for the beautiful gift of your Holy Spirit. May our lives be an open book to reflect your light to the world. Amen.

25

Pentecost: Unify
The Golden Rule
by Norman Rockwell

PASSAGE: Galatians 3:27–29 [23–29]

PURPOSE: When we look with eyes of faith, we see brothers and sisters in Christ.

PREPARATION: Art selection
The Golden Rule, 1961; the Norman Rockwell Museum of Stockbridge, Massachusetts. *Imaging the Word—An Arts and Lectionary Resource, Volume 1, 222.*

In his oil on canvas of *The Golden Rule*, the artist creates a tableau of the human family representing a respect for all cultures and races.

Norman Rockwell, 1894–1978, was a successful American illustrator who painted a realistic portrait of American society.

TEACHING TOOL: Ice cube tray, tea kettle, and water glass

PRESENTATION:
(Display the ice cube tray, tea kettle, and water glass.) How are these items alike and how are they different? *(Allow the participants to suggest similarities and differences such as "they all contain water" or "they are each different shapes.")* Even when things are different, we can find common ways to think about them, right? Does that work for people, too? *(As time permits, ask how the participants are alike as well as different.)* The bottom line is that—no matter how different we all are—we are all human beings, we are all God's children.

American illustrator Norman Rockwell seemed to have a knack for looking at human beings and seeing how we are all alike. For forty-seven years, he created paintings for the cover of one of America's most popular magazines, *The Saturday Evening Post.* On April 1, 1961, the magazine published this illustration of Norman Rockwell's entitled, *The Golden Rule. (If possible, hold up or display a print of* THE GOLDEN RULE.*)* What do you notice about this artwork? *(Invite and encourage responses to the art.)* The Golden Rule is the phrase we use to describe the words of Jesus: "Do unto others as you would have them do unto you." In this painting, Norman Rockwell shows us a human family portrait. He reminds us that we always have more in common than we sometimes remember.

This painting also helps us remember the message of Pentecost—that we are all one in Christ. The church is not unified because Christians are all just the same; we are unified because we are filled with the same Spirit of God. As Christians, we understand that God is the Creator of us all, that Jesus came to earth to save us from sin, and that the Holy Spirit is God's ever-present energy that empowers us to live in ways that honor God. We begin to honor God when we honor the people that God has created. By the Holy Spirit's power, we can begin not just to say the words to the Golden Rule, but to paint the picture with our lives.

PRAYER:
Dear God, thank you for the wide variety of people in your world. Help us to treat all of them as we want to be treated ourselves. Amen.

26
Pentecost: Celebrate
All Creatures Celebrate
by Hildegard of Bingen

PASSAGE: Romans 12:5

PURPOSE: In celebrating the gift of the Spirit, we discover that we must also celebrate one another.

PREPARATION: Art selection
All Creatures Celebrate, Illumination 15, 1165; Matthew Fox, *Illuminations of Hildegard of Bingen* (Santa Fe: Bear & Co., 1985). *Imaging the Word—An Arts and Lectionary Resource*, Volume 2, 264, 265.

In her illumination, *All Creatures Celebrate*, Hildegard of Bingen depicts the unity found in God's Holy Spirit as nine choirs of angels radiate in a mandala, a concentric vision of the divine.

Hildegard of Bingen, 1098–1179, abbess of a large Benedictine abbey, was a theologian, preacher, healer, scientist, artist, composer, poet, and author who, today, is considered one of the most creative and innovative Christian mystics of all time.

TEACHING TOOL: Circle

PRESENTATION:
(Hold up a drawing of a circle.) Have you ever drawn one of these? I am certain you have. What is this shape called? *(Pause for an answer.)* Yes, this shape is called a "circle." In the early language of human beings called "Sanskrit," this form was called a "mandala" *(mun´-de-le).* A mandala is also a symbol of the universe, representing all creation as

one in God. So a circle—or mandala—is an excellent symbol to use on Pentecost. Who knows what happened on the first Pentecost? *(Allow volunteers to retell the story, prompting or adding details from Acts 2:1–13.)* The story of Pentecost is the powerful account of the birth of the Christian church. The church exists today because God fills believers with the power of the Holy Spirit so that we may go out into the world and tell everyone of the saving gift of Jesus' love.

An artist from long ago named Hildegard of Bingen spent her life telling people about God's love. She was an abbess, a leader in a convent, a place where women live and work together for God. But Hildegard was a woman who believed that God worked through all people—male and female, young and old, rich and poor. She used her many gifts in art, music, poetry, and speaking to challenge people to discover God's power in life. Even though she did not have formal education, Hildegard wrote books to explain the visions God gave her of the way the world should celebrate life. She also illustrated her books with pictures called illuminations. One illumination from her book *Scivia* is a mandala called by some *All Creatures Celebrate* and by others *The Choirs of Angels. (If possible, hold up or display a print of* ALL CREATURES CELEBRATE.*)* What do you notice about this artwork? *(Invite or encourage responses to the art.)*

As human beings, we often draw lines rather than circles. We draw lines to separate ourselves from other people, to point out our differences or to keep others away from what is "ours." In this mandala, all of the colors and patterns draw the viewer's eye to the center. The circles within circles suggest that all the angels are looking toward God. They are drawn together in a celebration of oneness. That is what Hildegard believed was God's message to her. That is the message God sends to us as we celebrate Pentecost. We are one in God's spirit—no lines of separation—only greater and greater circles that celebrate God's unifying love.

PRAYER:
Dear God, thank you for the vision of Pentecost that we may all be one in your love. Help us to draw others into your circle. Amen.

27

Trinity Sunday: Welcome
Icon of the Trinity by Andrei Rublev

PASSAGE: Matthew 10:40, 42

PURPOSE: By accepting the invitation to worship God as a Trinity, we experience welcome.

PREPARATION: Art selection
Icon of the Trinity, ca. 1411; Tretyakov Gallery, Moscow, Russia.
Imaging the Word—An Arts and Lectionary Resource, Volume 2, 232.

In the rich colors of egg tempera on wood found in the Icon of the Trinity, the artist paints the symbolic understanding of the three persons of God.

Andrei Rublev, c. 1360–1430, was a Russian icon painter.

TEACHING TOOL: Paint strip of white samples

PRESENTATION:

What color is white? (Allow some discussion; then hold up the paint strip of choices.) We think of white as one shade of color, and yet look at all the different colors of white we have on this paint sample. Did you know that white actually reflects the light of all of the visible rays of the color spectrum? When we see a rainbow, we are seeing the white light broken into its parts. How wonderful that we can see all the different colors! And yet, how dazzling white can be! Artists have always combined the use of color and light to create the beauty of their images. The artistic images called "icons" combine color and light to make visible the invisible message of God's love.

An icon by a Russian artist of the 1400s, Andrei Rublev, called Icon of the Trinity, portrays the beautiful mystery of God as Father, Son, and Holy Spirit. (If possible, hold up or display a print of ICON OF THE

TRINITY.) What do you notice about this artwork? (*Invite or encourage responses to the art.*) Those who study icons like this one look carefully at the colors and the symbols that the artist includes in the painting. The colors and symbols can be "doors" to our understanding, not only of the painting, but also of God. Of course, the three angels represent God as Father, Son, and Holy Spirit. Not everyone who interprets the icon agrees which figure is which. However, the figure who holds the staff with two hands and sits in front of the house can be thought of as God the Father, the all-powerful Creator whose house has "many mansions." Although each figure wears the spiritual color blue, this figure's blue robe is mostly hidden from view by the almost translucent outer garment. The other figures also lean their heads toward this one, suggesting that they are listening. The central figure in front of the tree has a robe that is brown, like the earth. Since Jesus came to earth and was crucified on a tree, this figure can be seen as Christ. The third figure's blue robe is covered by green, the color of life and growing. The Holy Spirit brings God's power to earth, symbolized by the mountain behind this angel. So each figure represents one part of our understanding of God. And together they symbolize the Trinity. That's a lot of symbolism! Even looking at the three figures, we still have trouble understanding such a mystery.

Rublev was inspired to paint this icon from the story in Genesis when Abraham and Sarah entertained three angels. Rublev came to see those three angels as the three representations of our one God. The white color of the light around each angel's head and the white of the table represent the blinding light of God that is beyond our ability to see and understand—just like we can't see all the different colors of light in the color white. (*Hold up the paint strip.*) In the Trinity, God's love is broken into three persons we can recognize. And, most importantly, God invites us to join in conversation. See the open spot at the table of light? Each viewer of the icon has the opportunity to join the three visitors and to experience the mystery of God's love.

PRAYER:
Dear God, thank you for the beauty of light that can help us see the mystery of your love. Amen.

28
World Communion Sunday: Sow
The Sower by Vincent van Gogh

PASSAGE: Matthew 13:3

PURPOSE: On World Communion Sunday we are challenged to remember that God's vision is for the whole world to be covered with the seeds of love.

PREPARATION: Art selection
The Sower, 1888; *Rijksmuseum Kroeller-Mueller*, Otterlo, The Netherlands. *Imaging the Word—An Arts and Lectionary Resource, Volume 2*, 238, 239; Poster Set Two.

In the oil on canvas representation of *The Sower*, the artist uses vibrant colors and thick strokes to fill the canvas with dynamic movement.

Vincent van Gogh
Dutch post-Impressionist painter Vincent van Gogh, 1853–90, sought to bring a greater emotional freedom in painting, developing a unique style using thick brush strokes and vibrant colors to capture his vision of a dynamic world.

TEACHING TOOL: Wildflower seeds and sower's canvas bag

PRESENTATION:
Do you know what I have in this bag? (*Allow the participants to see and/or touch the seeds in the bag.*) Yes! These are seeds of all different kinds. If we plant them in the ground, we will get a wonderful variety of wildflowers. Can you picture what that might look like? (*Let the participants suggest colors or types of flowers.*) A wildflower garden can

be a beautiful riot of colors and fragrances. Different colors and different types of flowers make a wildflower garden something special. We could make quite a bouquet! And if we were artists, we could paint a beautiful still life picture of our flowers.

Some artists are famous for creating still life paintings. One Dutch artist named Vincent van Gogh wanted to do something more than paint still life, however. He wanted to bring more color and freedom to paintings than the artists who were famous during his lifetime. He was also a very religious man who wanted to help spread God's Word to others. Maybe that's why he wanted to paint his vision of Jesus' parable of the "Sower and the Seed." Do you know that story? *(Briefly retell or invite the listeners to help tell the parable found in Matthew 13:3–8.)* Here is Vincent van Gogh's vision of that story. *(If possible, hold up or display a print of* THE SOWER.*)* What do you notice about this artwork? *(Invite or encourage responses to the art.)* For van Gogh, the color yellow symbolized faith, triumph, and love. The deep blue represented the divine. He combined these colors so that they seem to move together and show the relationship of all living things.

On this World Communion Sunday, we remember that God's vision is for all Christians to work together to sow the seeds of God's love all over the world. In order to accomplish God's mission, we will need to be bold, we will need to work together, and we will need to keep in front of us a vision of the beauty of all people and places. Maybe we can begin by planting a wildflower garden to remind us of the varied beauty of God's world and God's love for each unique person.

PRAYER:
Dear God, thank you for your love that makes each one of us unique. Help us to scatter your seeds of love around the world. Amen.

29
All Saints' Day: Express
Allerheiligen (All Saints')
by Wassily Kandinsky

PASSAGE: Revelation 14:13

PURPOSE: The saints of God are called to express their joy in recognition of God's triumph over death.

PREPARATION: Art selection
Allerheiligen (All Saints'), 1911; *Stadtische Galerie im Lenbachhaus*, Munich, Germany. *Imaging the Word—An Arts and Lectionary Resource, Volume 3*, 64, 65, Poster Set Three.

In this oil on glass expressionist painting, the artist uses bold color and forms to represent the joy of resurrection when the saints arise.

Russian Expressionist painter Wassily Kandinsky, 1866–1944, was one of the most important artists of the twentieth century, and one of the first to move toward pure abstractionist painting, believing that color and form could convey not only his deepest feelings, but also spiritual meanings.

TEACHING TOOL: Comic book

PRESENTATION:
Do you ever read books like this? (*Hold up a sample comic book.*) At one time in America, most kids had collections of comic books with lots of heroes. More than the stories, the illustrations captured the imaginations and hearts of millions of readers. The bold and colorful

pictures themselves really told the story. There might be a word like "Bop!" or "Bif!" or "Shazam!" However, the impact of the artwork was much more powerful than the words.

We may not connect comic books with serious artists; yet, modern painters also began to experiment with bold color and abstract images. The goal of an abstract image is to help the viewer experience an emotion or a spiritual truth. One of the earliest Expressionist artists to experiment with abstract images was Wassily Kandinsky. Born in Russia, Kandinsky later studied in Germany where he began to explore how color and form could create meaning without the need for a story or specific figures. He wanted to use his artwork to convey his own deepest feelings, even his spiritual understandings. *(If possible, hold up or display a print of* ALLERHEILGEN (ALL SAINTS).*)* What do you notice about this artwork? *(Invite or encourage responses to the art.)* Allerheilgen means "All Saints" in German. Kandinsky's artwork seems to present a joyful expression of God's gathering in of all the saints. We don't need words to know in this painting that God is victorious over all things—even death.

On All Saints Day in the church year, we joyously celebrate all those Christians who have come before us. When we think of the lives of those who have trusted God and followed the way of Jesus, we might imagine an amazing scene like the one Kandinsky painted for us. We wouldn't say "shazam!" but we might say, "Hallelujah!" as we think of the heroes of the faith called saints. Of course, if All Saints Day is to continue into the future, then we must be willing to express our faith, to live out God's call on our lives, so that we can join the celebration of the faithful in God's eternity.

PRAYER:
Dear God, thank you for the saints who have shown us your power. Help us to express our faith so that your story may continue to be told. Amen.

30
Reign of Christ Sunday: Rule

Last Judgment by Gislebertus

PASSAGE: Matthew 25:40b

PURPOSE: On Reign of Christ Sunday, Christians are called to assess their efforts in bringing Christ's reign to earth, measured by their help of others.

PREPARATION: Art selection
Last Judgment, ca. 1120–35; Cathedral, Autun, Franc. *Imaging the Word—An Arts and Lectionary Resource, Volume 3*, 77.

Decorating the tympanum and lintel on the west portal of the cathedral in Autun, France, the limestone sculpture *Last Judgment*, details the final accounting of human beings, with the righteous saints and angels on Christ's right and with the unrighteous beings escorted to hell on Christ's left.

Although Medieval artisans usually remained anonymous, Gislebertus, the sculptor of Last Judgment, proudly signs his work so that at least his name remains to connect his artistry with the memorable scene carved on the cathedral's tympanum.

TEACHING TOOL: Report card

PRESENTATION:
Have any of you ever gotten a report card? What is a report card? (*Let volunteers explain what a report card means to them.*) Report cards let us know if we have done the work and learned the lessons that were expected of us. What if there were report cards for Christians? Does God give out report cards? (*Puzzle over that idea as time allows.*) Well, scripture teaches us that, at some point, time on earth will come to

an end. There will be no more opportunity to learn the lessons Jesus came to teach us. The name we use for the coming of that day is not "report card day" but the "last judgment."

In the Middle Ages, people often presented the idea of the last judgment as a scary time. One cathedral in France has a sculpture of the final judgment on the tympanum, the arch just above the doorway to the church. Every time people entered the cathedral they had to walk under that scene. *(If possible, hold up or display a print of* LAST JUDGMENT.*)* What do you notice about this artwork? *(Invite or encourage responses to the art.)* The sculptor who carved this scene must have been proud of his work. Most sculptures of this time period are not signed, but the *Last Judgment* on this tympanum carries the name Gislebertus. Perhaps it was such a vivid presentation of the end of time that people wanted to know who created such a masterpiece. That sculpture would be a vivid reminder of a coming report card!

Before we get a report card it's important for us to know what we were expected to learn, right? What do you think Jesus would expect Christians to know? Maybe the Scriptures help us to understand how Jesus would grade us. On Reign of Christ Sunday, we often read the scripture from Matthew 25 about the last judgment when Jesus will divide those who deserve the reward of heaven from those who do not. *(Retell or discuss Matthew 25:31–46.)* The parable that Jesus told suggests that we will be judged based on how we have helped other people. The Christian who deserves the reward of heaven is one who has cared for those in need just as if that person were Jesus himself. On Reign of Christ Sunday, we remember that we do have to answer to Christ for how we live our lives. The important thing to remember is that Jesus is a good teacher. If we follow and learn how to treat other people as Jesus teaches, we won't have to worry about the end of time. Jesus will reveal to us that our good deeds were done for him.

PRAYER:
Dear God, thank you for sending Jesus to teach us the way to live that leads to eternal life. Help us to learn the lesson of love each day. Amen.

Art Selections
Artists

Bingen, Hildegard of. *All Creatures Celebrate*, Illumination 15. 1165. Fox, Matthew. *Illuminations of Hildegard of Bingen* (Santa Fe: Bear & Co., 1985.). *Imaging the Word*, Volume 2, 264, 265.

PENTECOST: CELEBRATE

Buonarotti, Michelangelo. *Original Sin and Expulsion from Paradise (Fall of Man)*, 1509–10. Sistine Chapel, Vatican City. *Imaging the Word*, Volume 2, 149.

FIRST SUNDAY IN LENT: KNOW

Chagall, Marc. *Klageleid des Jeremias*, 1956. ARS, New York. *Imaging the Word*, Volume 3, 177.

FIFTH SUNDAY IN LENT: ADOPT

Dali, Salvador. *Girl Standing at the Window*, 1925. Museo d'Arts Contemporanea, Madrid, Spain. *Imaging the Word*, Volume 3, 19, 78, 83.

FIRST SUNDAY IN ADVENT: KEEP AWAKE

di Bondone, Giotto. *The Meeting of the Virgin and Elizabeth*, after 1306. la capella degli Scrovegni (Arena Chapel), Padua, Italy. *Imaging the Word*, Volume 1, 89.

FOURTH SUNDAY IN ADVENT: EMBRACE

da Caravaggio, Michelangelo Merisi. *The Incredulity of St. Thomas*, 1601–02. Uffizi Gallery, Florence, Italy. *Imaging the Word*, Volume 1, 191.

EASTER: BELIEVE

Gislebertus. *Last Judgment*, ca. 1120–35. Cathedral, Autun, France. *Imaging the Word*, Volume 3, 77.

REIGN OF CHRIST SUNDAY: RULE

Giuliani, John. *Hopi Virgin Mother and Child*, 1992. Burlington, Vermont: Bridge Building Images. *Imaging the Word*, Volume 3, 109. Poster Set Three.

CHRISTMAS: EMBODY

Haring, Keith. *Altarpiece: The Life of Christ*, 1989. Grace Episcopal Cathedral, San Francisco, California. *Imaging the Word*, Volume 3, 172, 173.

FOURTH SUNDAY IN LENT: SEND

Kandinsky, Wassily. *Allerheiligen (All Saints')*, 1911. Stadtische Galerie im Lenbachhaus, Munich, Germany. *Imaging the Word*, Volume 3, 64, 65. Poster Set Three.

ALL SAINTS' DAY: EXPRESS

Kussudiardja, Bagong. *The Ascension*, 1998. Takenaka, Masao, and Ron O'Grady.

The Bible Through Asian Eyes. Auckland, New Zealand: Pace Publishing in association with the Asian Christian Art Association, 1991, 165.). *Imaging the Word, Volume 2,* 202.

ASCENSION DAY: DANCE

LaDuke, Betty. *Guatemala: Procession,* 1978. Artist's Collection, Ashland, Oregon. *Imaging the Word, Volume 3,* 181.

PALM/PASSION SUNDAY: PROCESS

LaFarge, John. *Visit of Nicodemus to Christ,* 1880. National Museum of American Art, Smithsonian Institution, Washington, D.C. *Imaging the Word, Volume 2,* 155.

SECOND SUNDAY IN LENT: ACKNOWLEDGE

Manuscript Illumination. *Receiving Ashes,* ca. 1450, from *The Hours of the Duchess of Bourgogne. Musee Conde,* Chantilly, France. *Imaging the Word, Volume 2,* 145.

ASH WEDNESDAY: REPENT

Mondrian, Piet. *Red Amaryllis with Blue Background,* ca. 1907. The Museum of Modern Art, New York. *Imaging the Word, Volume 3,* 91.

THIRD SUNDAY IN ADVENT: SPRING UP

Nolde, Emil. *Christ Among the Children,* 1910. The Museum of Modern Art, New York. *Imaging the Word, Volume 1,* 20, 21. Poster Set One.

INTRODUCTION

O'Keefe, Georgia. *Black Cross, New Mexico.* Art Institute of Chicago, Chicago, Illinois. *Imaging the Word, Volume 3,* 188.

GOOD FRIDAY: HELP

Pourbus, Franz the Elder. *Sermon of St. John the Baptist,* 1569. *Musee des Beaux-Arts,* Valenciennes, France. *Imaging the Word, Volume 1,* 81.

SECOND SUNDAY IN ADVENT: PREPARE

Raphael. *The Transfiguration,* ca. 1519–20. *Pinacoteca,* Vatican Museums, Vatican State, Italy. *Imaging the Word, Volume 3,* 149.

EPIPHANY—TRANSFIGURATION: TRANSFORM

Rockwell, Norman. *The Golden Rule,* 1961. The Norman Rockwell Museum of Stockbridge, Massachusetts. *Imaging the Word, Volume 1,* 222.

PENTECOST: UNIFY

Rubens, Peter Paul. *The Adoration of the Magi,* 1624. *Musees Royaux des Beaux Arts,* Antwerp, Belgium. *Imaging the Word, Volume 1,* 109, 110.

EPIPHANY—MAGI: REVEAL

Rublev, Andrei. *Icon of the Trinity,* ca. 1411. *Tretyakov* Gallery, Moscow, Russia. *Imaging the Word, Volume 2,* 232.

TRINITY SUNDAY: WELCOME

Ryder, Albert P. *Christ Appearing to Mary,* 1885. National Museum of American Art, Smithsonian Institution, Washington, D.C. *Imaging the Word, Volume 1,* 186.

EASTER: REJOICE

Tanner, Henry Ossawa. *Angels Appearing Before the Shepherds,* 1910. National Museum of American Art, Smithsonian Institution, Washington, D.C. *Imaging the Word, Volume 1,* 98, 99. Poster Set One.

CHRISTMAS: WONDER

Tintoretto (Jacopo Robusti). *Last Supper,* 1592–94. Church of San Georgio

Maggiore, Venice, Italy. *Imaging the Word, Volume 1*, 175.

HOLY THURSDAY: REFLECT

Unknown. *Jesus and the Samaritan Woman*, 350–400. Catacomb of *via Latina*, Rome, Italy. *Imaging the Word, Volume 2*, 157.

THIRD SUNDAY IN LENT: ASK

Unknown. *Pentecost from the Rabbula Gospel*, ca. mid-sixth century. Biblioteca Medicea Laurenziana, Florence, Italy. *Imaging the Word, Volume 2*, 208, 212. Poster Set Two.

PENTECOST: FILL

van Gogh, Vincent. *The Sower*, 1888. Rijksmuseum Kroeller-Mueller, Otterlo, The Netherlands. *Imaging the Word, Volume 2*, 238, 239. Poster Set Two.

WORLD COMMUNION SUNDAY: SOW

van Rijn, Rembrandt Harmensz. *Presentation of Christ in the Temple*, ca. 1627–28. Kunsthalle, Hamburg, Germany. *Imaging the Word, Volume 3*, 103.

CHRISTMAS: RECOGNIZE

Velazquez, Diego Rodriguez de Silva y. *The Moorish Kitchen Maid*, ca. 1620. National Gallery of Ireland, Dublin. *Imaging the Word, Volume 2*, 190, 191. Poster Set Two.

EASTER: LISTEN

West, Pheoris. *The Baptism of Jesus Christ*, 1993. Artist's Collection, Columbus, Ohio. *Imaging the Word, Volume 1*, 113. Poster Set One.

EPIPHANY—BAPTISM: CENTER

Art Selections
Titles

All Creatures Celebrate, Illumination 15, 1165. Bingen, Hildegard of. Fox, Matthew. *Illuminations of Hildegard of Bingen* (Santa Fe: Bear & Co., 1985.). *Imaging the Word, Volume 2*, 264, 265.
PENTECOST: CELEBRATE

Allerheiligen (All Saints'), 1911. Kandinsky, Wassily. *Stadtische Galerie im Lenbachhaus*, Munich, Germany. *Imaging the Word, Volume 3*, 64, 65. Poster Set Three.
ALL SAINTS' DAY: EXPRESS

Altarpiece: The Life of Christ, 1989. Haring, Keith. Grace Episcopal Cathedral, San Francisco, CA. *Imaging the Word, Volume 3*, 172, 173.
FOURTH SUNDAY IN LENT: SEND

Angels Appearing Before the Shepherds, 1910. Tanner, Henry Ossawa. National Museum of American Art, Smithsonian Institution, Washington, D.C. *Imaging the Word, Volume 1*, 98, 99. Poster Set One.
CHRISTMAS: WONDER

Black Cross, New Mexico. O'Keefe, Georgia. Art Institute of Chicago, Chicago, Illinois. *Imaging the Word, Volume 3*, 188.
GOOD FRIDAY: HELP

Christ Among the Children, 1910. Nolde, Emil. The Museum of Modern Art, New York. *Imaging the Word, Volume 1*, 20, 31. Poster Set One.
INTRODUCTION

Christ Appearing to Mary, 1885. Ryder, Albert P. National Museum of American Art, Smithsonian Institution, Washington, D.C. *Imaging the Word, Volume 1*, 186.
EASTER: REJOICE

Girl Standing at the Window, 1925. Dali, Salvador. Museo d'Arts Contemporanea, Madrid, Spain. *Imaging the Word, Volume 3*, 19, 78, 83.
FIRST SUNDAY IN ADVENT: KEEP AWAKE

Guatemala: Procession, 1978. LaDuke, Betty. Artist's Collection, Ashland, Oregon. *Imaging the Word, Volume 3*, 181.
PALM/PASSION SUNDAY: PROCESS

Hopi Virgin Mother and Child, 1992. Giuliani, John. Burlington, Vermont: Bridge Building Image. *Imaging the Word, Volume 3*, 109. Poster Set Three.
CHRISTMAS: EMBODY

Icon of the Trinity, ca. 1411. Rublev, Andrei. *Tretyakov* Gallery, Moscow, Russia. *Imaging the Word*, Volume 2, 232.
TRINITY SUNDAY: WELCOME

Jesus and the Samaritan Woman, 350–400. Catacomb of *via Latina*, Rome, Italy. *Imaging the Word*, Volume 2, 157.
THIRD SUNDAY IN LENT: ASK

Klageleid des Jeremias, 1956. Chagall, Marc. ARS, New York. *Imaging the Word*, Volume 3, 177.
FIFTH SUNDAY IN LENT: ADOPT

Last Judgment, ca. 1120–35. Gislebertus. Cathedral, Autun, France. *Imaging the Word*, Volume 3, 77.
REIGN OF CHRIST SUNDAY: RULE

Last Supper, 1592–94. Tintoretto (Jacopo Robusti). Church of *San Georgio Maggiore*, Venice, Italy. *Imaging the Word*, Volume 1, 175.
HOLY THURSDAY: REFLECT

Original Sin and Expulsion from Paradise (Fall of Man), 1509–10. Buonarotti, Michelangelo. Sistine Chapel, Vatican City. *Imaging the Word*, Volume 2, 149.
FIRST SUNDAY IN LENT: KNOW

Pentecost from the *Rabbula Gospel*, ca. mid-sixth century. *Biblioteca Medicea Laurenziana*, Florence, Italy. *Imaging the Word*, Volume 2, 208, 212. Poster Set Two.
PENTECOST: FILL

Presentation of Christ in the Temple, ca. 1627–28. van Rijn, Rembrandt Harmensz. *Kunsthalle*, Hamburg, Germany. *Imaging the Word*, Volume 3, 103.
CHRISTMAS: RECOGNIZE

Receiving Ashes, ca. 1450. Manuscript Illumination from *The Hours of the Duchess of Bourgogne*. Musee Conde, Chantilly, France. *Imaging the Word*, Volume 2, 145.
ASH WEDNESDAY: REPENT

Red Amaryllis with Blue Background, ca. 1907. Mondrian, Piet. The Museum of Modern Art, New York. *Imaging the Word*, Volume 3, 91.
THIRD SUNDAY IN ADVENT: SPRING UP

Sermon of St. John the Baptist, 1569. Pourbus, Franz the Elder. *Musee des Beaux-Arts*, Valenciennes, France. *Imaging the Word*, Volume 1, 81.
SECOND SUNDAY IN ADVENT: PREPARE

The Adoration of the Magi, 1624. Rubens, Peter Paul. *Musees Royaux des Beaux Arts*, Antwerp, Belgium. *Imaging the Word*, Volume 1, 109, 110.
EPIPHANY—MAGI: REVEAL

The Ascension, 1998. Kussudiardja, Bagong. Takenaka, Masao and Ron O'Grady. *The Bible Through Asian Eyes* (Auckland, New Zealand: Pace Publishing in association with the Asian Christian Art Association, 1991, 165.). *Imaging the Word*, Volume 2, 202.
ASCENSION DAY: DANCE

The Baptism of Jesus Christ, 1993. West, Pheoris. Artist's Collection, Columbus, Ohio. *Imaging the Word*, Volume 1, 113. Poster Set One.
EPIPHANY—BAPTISM: CENTER

The Golden Rule, 1961. Rockwell, Norman. The Norman Rockwell Museum of Stockbridge, Massachusetts. *Imaging the Word*, Volume 1, 222.
PENTECOST: UNIFY

The Incredulity of St. Thomas, 1601–02. Da Caravaggio, Michelangelo Merisi. Uffizi Gallery, Florence, Italy. *Imaging the Word, Volume 1*, 191.
EASTER: BELIEVE

The Meeting of the Virgin and Elizabeth, after 1306. di Bondone, Giotto. *la capella degli Scrovegni* (Arena Chapel), Padua, Italy. *Imaging the Word, Volume 1*, 89.
FOURTH SUNDAY IN ADVENT: EMBRACE

The Moorish Kitchen Maid, ca. 1620. Velazquez, Diego Rodriguez de Silva y. National Gallery of Ireland, Dublin. Imaging the Word, Volume 2, 190, 191. Poster Set Two.
EASTER: LISTEN

The Sower, 1888. van Gogh, Vincent. Rijksmuseum Kroeller-Mueller, Otterlo, The Netherlands. Imaging the Word, Volume 2, 238, 239. Poster Set Two.
WORLD COMMUNION SUNDAY: SOW

The Transfiguration, ca. 1519–20. Raphael. Pinacoteca, Vatican Museums, Vatican State, Italy. Imaging the Word, Volume 3, 149.
EPIPHANY—TRANSFIGURATION: TRANSFORM

Visit of Nicodemus to Christ, 1880. LaFarge, John. National Museum of American Art, Smithsonian Institution, Washington, D.C. Imaging the Word, Volume 2, 155.
SECOND SUNDAY IN LENT: ACKNOWLEDGE

Imaging the Word
Volumes 1, 2, 3

Volume 1

Volume 2

All Creatures Celebrate, Illumination 15, 1165. Bingen, Hildegard of. Fox, Matthew. *Illuminations of Hildegard of Bingen* (Santa Fe: Bear & Co., 1985.). Volume 2, 264, 265.

PENTECOST: CELEBRATE

Icon of the Trinity, ca. 1411. Rublev, Andrei. *Tretyakov* Gallery, Moscow, Russia. Volume 2, 232.

TRINITY SUNDAY: WELCOME

Jesus and the Samaritan Woman, 350–400. Unknown. Catacomb of *via Latina*, Rome, Italy. Volume 2, 157.

THIRD SUNDAY IN LENT: ASK

Original Sin and Expulsion from Paradise (Fall of Man), 1509–10. Buonarotti, Michelangelo. Sistine Chapel, Vatican City. Volume 2, 149.

FIRST SUNDAY IN LENT: KNOW

Pentecost from the Rabbula Gospel, ca. mid-sixth century. *Biblioteca Medicea Laurenziana*, Florence, Italy. Volume 2, 208, 212. Poster Set Two.

PENTECOST: FILL

Receiving Ashes, ca. 1450, from *The Hours of the Duchess of Bourgogne*. Manuscript Illustration. *Musee Conde*, Chantilly, France. Volume 2, 145.

ASH WEDNESDAY: REPENT

The Ascension, 1998. Kussudiardja, Bagong. Takenaka, Masao and Ron O'Grady. *The Bible Through Asian Eyes* (Auckland, New Zealand: Pace Publishing in association with the Asian Christian Art Association, 1991, 165.). Volume 2, 202.

ASCENSION DAY: DANCE

The Moorish Kitchen Maid, ca. 1620. Velazquez, Diego Rodriguez de Silva y. National Gallery of Ireland, Dublin, Ireland. Volume 2, 190, 191. Poster Set Two.

EASTER: LISTEN

The Sower, 1888. van Gogh, Vincent. Rijksmuseum Kroeller-Mueller, Otterlo, The Netherlands. Volume 2, 238, 239. Poster Set Two.

WORLD COMMUNION SUNDAY: SOW

Visit of Nicodemus to Christ, 1880.' LaFarge, John. National Museum of American Art, Smithsonian Institution, Washington, D.C. Volume 2, 155.

SECOND SUNDAY IN LENT: ACKNOWLEDGE

Volume 3

Allerheiligen (All Saints'), 1911. Kandinsky, Wassily. *Stadtische Galerie im Lenbachhaus*, Munich, Germany. Volume 3, 64, 65. Poster Set Three.

ALL SAINTS' DAY: EXPRESS

Altarpiece: The Life of Christ, 1989. Haring, Keith. Grace Episcopal Cathedral, San Francisco, CA. Volume 3, 172, 173.

FOURTH SUNDAY IN LENT: SEND

Black Cross, New Mexico. O'Keefe, Georgia. Art Institute of Chicago, Chicago, Illinois. Volume 3, 188.

GOOD FRIDAY: HELP

Girl Standing at the Window, 1925. Dali, Salvador. *Museo d'Arts Contemporanea*, Madrid, Spain. Volume 3, 19, 78, 83.
FIRST SUNDAY IN ADVENT: KEEP AWAKE
Guatemala: Procession, 1978. LaDuke, Betty. Artist's Collection, Ashland, Oregon. Volume 3, 181. Poster Set Three.
PALM/PASSION SUNDAY: PROCESS
Hopi Virgin Mother and Child, 1992. Giuliani, John. Bridge Building Images, Burlington, Vermont. Volume 3, 109. Poster Set Three.
CHRISTMAS: EMBODY
Klageleid des Jeremias, 1956. Chagall, Marc. ARS, New York. Volume 3, 177.
Fifth Sunday in Lent: Adopt
Last Judgment, ca 1120–35. Gislebertus. Cathedral, Autun, France. Volume 3, 77.
REIGN OF CHRIST SUNDAY: RULE
Presentation of Christ in the Temple, ca. 1627–28. van Rijn, Rembrandt Harmensz. *Kunsthalle*, Hamburg, Germany. Volume 3, 103.
CHRISTMAS: RECOGNIZE
Red Amaryllis with Blue Background, ca. 1907. Mondrian, Piet. The Museum of Modern Art, New York. Volume 3, 91.
THIRD SUNDAY IN ADVENT: SPRING UP
The Transfiguration, ca. 1519–20. Raphael. *Pinacoteca*, Vatican Museums, Vatican State, Italy. Volume 3, 149.
EPIPHANY—TRANSFIGURATION: TRANSFORM

Imaging the Word Poster Sets One, Two, Three

Poster Set One

Angels Appearing Before the Shepherds, 1910. Tanner, Henry Ossawa. National Museum of American Art, Smithsonian Institution, Washington, D.C. *Imaging the Word*, Volume 1, 98, 99.
CHRISTMAS: WONDER

Christ Among the Children, 1910. Nolde, Emil. The Museum of Modern Art, New York. *Imaging the Word*, Volume 1, 20, 31. Poster Set One.
INTRODUCTION

The Baptism of Jesus Christ, 1993. West, Pheoris. Artist's Collection, Columbus, Ohio. *Imaging the Word*, Volume 1, 113. Poster Set One.
EPIPHANY—BAPTISM: CENTER

Poster Set Two

Pentecost from the Rabbula Gospel, ca. mid-sixth century. *Biblioteca Medicea Laurenziana*, Florence, Italy. *Imaging the Word*, Volume 2, 208, 212. Poster Set Two.
PENTECOST: FILL

The Moorish Kitchen Maid, ca. 1620. Velazquez, Diego Rodriguez de Silva y. National Gallery of Ireland, Dublin. *Imaging the Word*, Volume 2, 190, 191. Poster Set Two.
EASTER: LISTEN

The Sower, 1888. van Gogh, Vincent. Rijksmuseum Kroeller-Mueller, Otterlo, The Netherlands. *Imaging the Word*, Volume 2, 238, 239. Poster Set Two.
WORLD COMMUNION SUNDAY: SOW

Poster Set Three

Allerheiligen (All Saints'), 1911. Kandinsky, Wassily. *Stadtische Galerie im Lenbachhaus*, Munich, Germany. *Imaging the Word*, Volume 3, 64, 65. Poster Set Three.
ALL SAINTS' DAY: EXPRESS

Guatemala: Procession, 1978. LaDuke, Betty. Artist's Collection, Ashland, Oregon. *Imaging the Word*, Volume 3, 181. Poster Set Three.
PALM/PASSION SUNDAY: PROCESS

Hopi Virgin Mother and Child, 1992. Giuliani, John. Bridge Building Images, Burlington, Vermont. *Imaging the Word*, Volume 3, 109. Poster Set Three.
CHRISTMAS: EMBODY

Scripture Cross-References

Hebrew Scriptures

Genesis 3:3–5—First Sunday in Lent: Know
Psalm 22:1–2—Good Friday: Help
Psalm 51:10–12—Ash Wednesday: Repent
Isaiah 61:11—Third Sunday in Advent: Spring Up
Jeremiah 31:33b—Fifth Sunday in Lent: Adopt

Christian Scriptures

Matthew 2:11–12 [1–12]—Epiphany—Magi: Reveal
Matthew 10:40, 42—Trinity Sunday: Welcome
Matthew 13:3—World Communion Sunday: Sow
Matthew 25:40b—Reign of Christ Sunday: Rule
Mark 9:2, 7–8—Epiphany—Transfiguration: Transform
Mark 9:35–37 [30–37]—Introduction
Mark 11:9–11a—Palm/Passion Sunday: Process
Mark 13:35–37—First Sunday in Advent: Keep Awake
Luke 1:39–42 [39–55]—Fourth Sunday in Advent: Embrace
Luke 2:13–14 [1–20]—Christmas: Wonder
Luke 2:26, 36a, 38—Christmas: Recognize
Luke 3:2b–4 [1–6]—Second Sunday in Advent: Prepare
Luke 3:21–22 [15–17, 21–22]—Epiphany—Baptism: Center
Luke 24:35—Easter: Listen
John 1:16—Christmas: Embody
John 3:1–3—Second Sunday in Lent: Acknowledge
John 3:16–17—Fourth Sunday in Lent: Send
John 4:7–10—Third Sunday in Lent: Ask
John 14:19–20—Ascension Day: Dance
John 20:15–16 [1–18]—Easter: Rejoice
John 20:19 [19–31]—Easter: Believe
Acts 2:1, 4—Pentecost: Fill
Romans 12:5—Pentecost: Celebrate
1 Corinthians 11:23–26—Holy Thursday: Reflect
Galatians 3:27–29 [23–29]—Pentecost: Unify
Revelation 14:13—All Saints' Day: Express

Teaching Tool
Cross-References

Alarm clock—First Sunday in Advent: Keep Awake
Apple (artificial)—First Sunday in Lent: Know
Amaryllis—Third Sunday in Advent: Spring Up
Bread—Easter: Listen
Business card—Second Sunday in Lent: Acknowledge
Calligraphy pen and gold ink—Pentecost: Fill
Circle—Pentecost: Celebrate
Comic book—All Saints' Day: Express
Drawing compass and T-square—Epiphany—Baptism: Center
Easter plants or spring bouquet—Easter: Rejoice
Egg—Christmas: Embody
Feathers—Ascension Day: Dance
Gift Box containing figures of the three Wise Men—Epiphany—Magi: Reveal
Graffiti wall—Fourth Sunday In Lent: Send
Halo—Holy Thursday: Reflect
Hour glass—Ash Wednesday: Repent
Ice cube tray, tea kettle, and water glass—Pentecost: Unify
JESUS optical illusion—Epiphany—Transfiguration: Transform
Litmus paper and acid and base solutions such as ammonia, baking soda and water,
    lemon juice, and white vinegar—Easter: Believe
Magnifying glass—Christmas: Recognize
Mask—Palm/Passion Sunday: Process
Music box mechanism—Christmas: Wonder
Paint strip of white samples—Trinity Sunday: Welcome
Pulley—Third Sunday in Lent: Ask
Report card—Reign of Christ Sunday: Rule
Scroll—Fifth Sunday in Lent: Adopt
Travel kit—Second Sunday in Advent: Prepare
Trowel—Fourth Sunday in Advent: Embrace
Veil, black—Good Friday: Help
Wildflower seeds and sower's canvas bag—World Communion Sunday: Sow

About the Authors

Phyllis Vos Wezeman

Phyllis Vos Wezeman is president of Active Learning Associates, Inc., and director of Christian Nurture at First Presbyterian Church in South Bend, Indiana. Phyllis has served as adjunct faculty in the Education Department at Indiana University and the Department of Theology at the University of Notre Dame. She has taught at the Saint Petersburg (Russia) State University and the Shanghai (China) Teacher's University. Phyllis, who holds an M.S. in Education from Indiana University, is a recipient of three "Distinguished Alumnae Awards" and the Catholic Library Association's Aggiornamento Award. Author or coauthor of numerous articles and books, Phyllis and her husband, Ken, have three children and three grandsons.

Anna L. Liechty

Ann Liechty is a National Board Certified teacher and chair of the English Department at Plymouth High School in Indiana. She has also worked as a religious education volunteer, teaching all levels, directing Sunday morning and youth programming, consulting with congregations about their educational ministry, and writing a wide variety of religious education materials. She serves as vice president of Active Learning Associates, Inc. Ann lives in Plymouth, Indiana, with her husband, Ron, a retired pastor. They have five children and ten grandchildren.

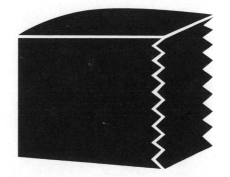

OTHER BOOKS FROM THE PILGRIM PRESS

TELL ME A STORY
30 Children's Sermons Based on Best-Loved Books
Phyllis Vos Wezeman and Anna L. Liechty
ISBN 0-8298-1635-6/paper/96 pages/$12.00

WIPE THE TEARS
30 Children's Sermons on Death
Phyllis Vos Wezeman, Anna L. Liechty, and Kenneth R. Wezeman
ISBN 0-8298-1520-1/paper/96 pages/$10.00

TASTE THE BREAD
30 Children's Sermons on Communion
Phyllis Vos Wezeman, Anna L. Liechty, and Kenneth R. Wezeman
ISBN 0-8298-1519-8/paper/96 pages/$10.00

TOUCH THE WATER
30 Children's Sermons on Baptism
Phyllis Vos Wezeman, Anna L. Liechty, Kenneth R. Wezeman
ISBN 0-8298-1518-X/112 pages/paper/$10.00

PLANTINGS SEEDS OF FAITH
Virginia H. Loewen
ISBN 0-8298-1473-6/96 pages/paper/$10.00

GROWING SEEDS OF FAITH
Virginia H. Loewen
ISBN 0-8298-1488-4/96 pages/paper/$10.00

THE BROWN BAG
Jerry Marshall Jordan
ISBN 0-8298-0411-0/117 pages/paper/$9.95

SMALL WONDERS
Sermons for Children
Glen E. Rainsley
ISBN 0-8298-1252-0/104 pages/paper/$12.95

TIME WITH OUR CHILDREN
Stories for Use in Worship, Year B
Dianne E. Deming
ISBN 0-8298-0952-X/182 pages/paper/$9.95

TIME WITH OUR CHILDREN
Stories for Use in Worship, Year C
Dianne E. Deming
ISBN 0-8298-0953-8/157 pages/paper/$9.95

To order these or any other books from The Pilgrim Press call or write to:
The Pilgrim Press
700 Prospect Avenue East, Cleveland, Ohio 44115-1100
Phone orders: 1-800-537-3394 • Fax orders: 216-736-2206
Please include shipping charges of $4.00 for the first book and $0.75 for each additional book.
Or order from our web sites at www.pilgrimpress.com and www.ucpress.com.
Prices subject to change without notice.